This Doesn't Feel Like Love

ROGER AND MARCIA LAMB

This Doesn't Feel Like Love

Trusting God
When Bad Things Happen

DPI
DISCIPLESHIP
PUBLICATIONS
INTERNATIONAL

One Merrill Street
Woburn, MA 01801
1-800-727-8237 • FAX 617-937-3889

This Doesn't Feel Like Love

©1996 by Discipleship Publications International
One Merrill Street, Woburn, MA 01801

Cover design : Chris Costello
Interior layout: Chris Costello and Laura Root

Printed in the United States of America

ISBN 1-884553-82-6

Dedication

To our children, Christie, Michael and David. You did not ask to take this journey with us; although without you, the journey would not have been as eventful and joyfully fulfilling as it was and as it now is. Knowing that God has his purpose for you, as well as for Mom and Dad, we love you and respect each of you for how you have turned "bad things" into good things!

To our friends, Bob and Patricia Gempel and all the HOPE Worldwide workers. Your sacrificial lives have inspired us and rekindled a depth of compassion that we all need. You have put sweat, blood and tears into your "living legacy" of Helping Other People Everywhere. Thank you.

Contents

PART 3
THE LAZARUS CLUB

Acknowledgments

To God, our Father and master potter, we thank you for creating us and re-creating us. Thank you for revealing your great love to us. We want to give you all the praise and gratitude you deserve as we attempt to reveal your great love to all your children.

Thank you to our family for the great physical and emotional support you have given to us. We survived and even thrived because of your love. Thank you Chester and Irene Lamb and Paul and Ruth Marks, our parents, who blazed a trail of faith for us. Thank you to our brothers and sisters and their spouses for your lifelong love and friendship. Thank you Christie, Michael and David for enriching our lives far beyond what we deserve.

To our many physicians, our deepest thanks for letting God use your talents, skills and dedication to improve and save our lives. Our special thanks goes to: Dr. Theresa Vietti, Dr. Stanley Thiel, Dr. Jim O'Conner, Dr. John Lurrain, Dr. Robin Mitchell, Dr. Robert McClellen, Drs. Ken and Ann Lowey, Dr. Hardy Tillman, Dr. Mitchel Levine, Dr. Carol Englender, Dr. Lipshultz, Dr. Muffit Jensen, Dr. Karen Cheng and a host of others.

A special thanks goes to the unsung heroes at the ICC Benefits Administration office. Your tireless help has lifted a tremendous burden off our shoulders. You have given your best to so many. Our thanks seem so puny in comparison to your efforts.

Each individual member of our great church family is precious and dear to us. Thank you all for your prayers of faith, your serving hearts and your encouragement. Thanks especially to the Charleston, Champaign, Chicago, Boston and Los Angeles church families. Special thanks go to the "psalmists of the kingdom" (Arts and Entertainment ministries) whose songs and love have soothed our souls.

Working with the DPI staff has been the fulfillment of a dream. Tom and Sheila Jones have been soul mates to us since our very first meeting. They came to comfort us when Michael was diagnosed with leukemia. Our hearts were immediately bonded, not only by our love for God, but also by the shared experience of having a child with a life-threatening illness. (Their daughter, Corrie, had open-heart surgery as an infant at the same hospital in St. Louis.) I can think of no one else we have cried and laughed with more than Tom and Sheila. Marcia and Sheila, known by some as a comedy team, know how each other thinks so well that Sheila could have written this book instead of editing it. (After all her edits, she may be feeling that she did write this book!) Thanks also to the incredible staff at DPI. Kim Hanson, Janet O'Donnell, Jerri Newman and Chris Costello made writing this book feel like a work of love.

Thank you to all the "Lazarus Club" members, named and unnamed. Your lives give hope to so many, including us.

Thank you to all our personal support staff. Thank you Al and Gloria Baird and Bob and Pat Gempel who have continuously believed in us and given us great guidance; Tammy and John Woodward, directors and screenwriters, for recently coming into our lives to refresh our souls, as well as our writing styles; Cecil and Helen Wooten and David and Coleen Graham for keeping our feet on the ground while our heads were in the clouds, thank you!

The very fact that we can write this book from a victorious point of view is because of our dear friends and spiritual comrades to whom we owe our souls: Kip and Elena McKean, Marty and Chris Fuqua, and John and Nancy Mannel. Thank you for our eternity.

Foreword

Leukemia. Cancer. Endometriosis. Depression. Any *one* of these would test our faith! What about all of these in one family? This is what Roger and Marcia deal with in *This Doesn't Feel Like Love*. It has been said that you can waste some things, but don't waste your suffering. Roger and Marcia have not wasted their suffering, but have used these times of testing and struggle to inspire others to trust God and persevere through hard times. They didn't just survive their ordeals, they came through them as wiser people with a much stronger faith in God.

As disciples of Jesus, we often try to help someone who is struggling with a problem with which we are unable to relate. This is especially true if that person is more emotionally oriented than we are. Our advice can come across as cold, uncaring and insensitive. Roger and Marcia's insight is invaluable in helping those with both physical and emotional problems since Marcia not only won a major battle with cancer, but also overcame clinical depression. Too often we oversimplify the solutions to complex emotional problems by automatically classifying the problem as sin and the solution as repentance. The result is that we damage those people whose situations may involve chemical imbalance or other physiological causes. While always being alert to correct specific sin in someone's life, we must also grow in our compassion and discernment.

The Lambs heard it all, dealt with it all and overcame. We have known Roger, Marcia and their family personally through many of these struggles. Their lives today are a testimony to God's power. Even in times of weakness, they remembered their purpose and have influenced many to come into God's kingdom. Their character has been refined and their talents have been developed and polished to the glory of God. Their experiences are tremendously useful not only to those who are undergoing similar problems, but to those who want to understand and encourage others who are in the midst of any type of challenge. *This Doesn't Feel Like Love* is must reading.

Al and Gloria Baird
LOS ANGELES, CALIFORNIA

Introduction

Can God Be Good If Bad Things Keep Happening?

How does suffering fit into God's plan for our spiritual and character development? How does understanding suffering from God's perspective help us handle our own suffering? How do we handle suffering when it keeps on coming? These questions are at least as old as the book of Job, but still intensely relevant. In our quick-fix society, we have learned to tolerate a moderate amount of inconvenience, but if suffering goes beyond what we think reasonable, we are tempted to give in to discouragement, anger or distrust.

On television, two or three life crises can be resolved within thirty minutes to an hour. Even the mini-series show a resolution within six to eight hours of TV time. Microwave ovens and nutrition bars, computers and electronics, intercontinental flights and space travel have redefined our expectations. Some things God has set in motion cannot be rushed or they will be harmed: the birth of a baby, the changing of seasons, the blooming of a rose, true love and the harvest. Some of God's most majestic creations took time and pressure to create: the Grand Canyon, precious jewels, mountains and sea shores. In the same way, we cannot rush God when it comes to our suffering. It's all a necessary part of his creation and re-creation process.

Although we did not handle all our family's suffering as well as Job handled his, we did find anchors to hold to in the midst of our trials. Suffering is a part of life. Paul says we should rejoice in our sufferings (Romans 5). The writer of Hebrews says that we should endure hardship as discipline from God (Hebrews 12). God disciplines those whom he loves so that they may eventually share in his holiness. James tells us in chapter one that we should consider it pure joy whenever we face trials of many kinds. Throughout his letters, Peter refers to suffering. Knowing that life will involve suffering, even as a disciple, does help us not to be surprised by it.

The overriding theme is

Hold on.
Don't quit.
You are still "in process."
It will be worth the wait.

Peter tells us,

> Humble yourselves, therefore, under God's mighty hand
> that he may lift you up in due time. Cast all your anxiety on
> him because he cares for you....
> And the God of all grace, who called you to his eternal
> glory in Christ, after you have suffered a little while, will
> himself restore you and make you strong, firm and stead-
> fast. To him be the power for ever and ever. Amen.
>
> *1 Peter 5:6-7, 10-11*

Only God knows when our suffering has accomplished its purpose in our lives. Only God knows when we have learned the lessons that we need to learn from our suffering. In the meantime, he tells us to

> Be self-controlled and alert. Your enemy the devil prowls
> around like a roaring lion looking for someone to devour.
> Resist him, standing firm in the faith, because you know
> that your brothers throughout the world are undergoing
> the same kind of sufferings.
>
> *1 Peter 5:8-9*

In this book I will share our journey through the refining process of suffering. Having learned to expect and appreciate the process, I share some aspects with a lighthearted slant. In the first part of the book, I share our family's personal journey through our son's leukemia, my cancer and other faith challenges that taught us to appreciate "being in the refining fire." (I suppose another title for this section could be "Roast

Lamb.") The second section of the book reveals how following the Beatitudes through our suffering will give us guidance, and help us to become more like Jesus. I use the Beatitudes of Jesus for an "attitude adjustment." Finally, the last section contains stories of other disciples who have found a deeper appreciation of God's love through their suffering.

The outline of the book is God's; we just helped by "fleshing out" the stories for you. I know you will be blessed, even though the suffering you go through doesn't *feel* like love. In due time, God will use it to make you "strong, firm and steadfast."

Marcia Lamb

I don't know why you picked up this book. Perhaps you have just been wondering why bad things keep happening to good people—yourself or someone you love. Let me get right to the point. This book came out of our dealing with the same question. We want to help you wrestle with it.

Our son had just been pronounced cured of leukemia when my wife had radical, emergency surgery and radiation treatment for two of the worst kinds of cervical cancer known to medical science. Then our beautiful teenage daughter was struck with several chronic illnesses we had never heard of. We had already dealt with the question, "Why do bad things happen to good people?" Or so we thought. We had paid our dues, learned our lessons and withstood our tests. It was time to move on to the mountaintop and say good-bye to the valley of the shadow of death. But here was a different test, "Why do bad things *keep happening* to good people?" This book tells you the answers we found to that question and where we found them: in the Bible. If you are not open to that, please read on anyway.

I will never forget the eerie scene when the doctors and nurses gathered us in the doctors' lounge of St. Louis Children's Hospital and said, "Your son has leukemia." The lights were low and the entire group leaned forward anticipating our reaction. Their announcement was filled with such personal pain and concern, our hearts actually went out to them. They left to give Marcia and me a few moments alone. Up to that point, all we knew of leukemia was that Michael's best friend, Shane, our next-door neighbor's son, had died of it just eight months earlier. To us, leukemia was a death sentence.

The very next thought that came through the fog that had filled my mind was the phrase, "rejoice in our sufferings." Seldom in my life had I felt so clueless about a concept. That week, the chief resident, who was working with Michael, found out her mother had been diagnosed with cancer. I shared with her that I was determined to figure out what that strange phrase meant.

Marcia and I went on a quest while dealing with legal forms, bone marrows, spinal taps, chemotherapy, doctors' offices, laboratories, 300-mile trips to the hospital, financial and emotional stress, two other scared children and one incredibly brave and stubborn six-year-old. After Michael was pronounced cured, I thought we had found the answer; that is, until Marcia's doctor finally broke the news to us about her condition. Then it was back to school. This book is an exploration of the answers we found on those incredible journeys.

I have no doubt today that our personal lives, our marriage, our family relationships would be a disaster without God. The pressure that leukemia, uterine cancer and chronic illness put on our family revealed plenty of cracks in us. Marcia has done an incredible job of showing you what our family went through in the furnace of life. We are not special. We are just thankful for the people in our life who taught us to listen to God and to act on what we heard. Commit yourself to wrestle with the concept until you can rejoice in your sufferings. Your whole view of bad things and good people will change.

Roger Lamb

Part 1

The Lambs' Book of Life

1

Bad Things Happen

"I have told you these things, so that in me you may have peace. In this world you will have trouble. But take heart! I have overcome the world."

John 16:33

Trembling, I followed the procession of doctors and nurses down the long hallway. As we walked, I noticed room after room of pale, frail children hooked up to tubes and lines. I glanced hopefully toward the infant nursery where sweet blue- and pink-blanketed bassinets should have been, but there were only tubes, incubators and little faces of babies with cleft palates and other facial deformities.

We stepped into a room hushed and softened by shadowy lights. I was uncomfortable with the quietness because my thoughts were still on our son Michael and the intense pain he had endured for the past, seemingly endless weeks. His nightly screams had jarred us into futile attempts to apply hot packs to pain that could not be eased. As we soaked him in tubs of warm water, his teeth chattered from unrelieved agony.

Night after night, lumps were appearing and multiplying on his head, prompting our pediatrician to send us to St. Louis Children's Hospital. Our appointment with him was on Monday, May 11, 1981—Michael's sixth birthday. We stopped our preparations for the St. Louis trip long enough for his birthday party. Michael was excited with his new Star Wars Millennium Falcon, but at the same time, sad that Shane wasn't there. Shane, our next door neighbor's son, had died nine months earlier from leukemia.

Would Michael be here for a seventh birthday party? I wondered.

My thoughts were interrupted by the sound of our doctor's voice. Roger held my hand tightly. "Mr. and Mrs. Lamb, your son has leukemia." The words slapped our faces and left us stunned. Everything else the doctor said was muffled by the silent cries of our hearts. The doctors and nurses tried to console us. "The risks? Yes, we need to tell you the risks of giving him chemotherapy." Through the stinging tears we tried to read the papers we were to sign.

Could his death be worse than these risks?

"What are the percentages?" Roger asked.

"There are none. We don't like to talk about percentages."

The words weighed heavy. My knees were giving way as Roger pulled me to his side, and we prayed together with the doctors and nurses. I couldn't believe his strength. How could he be so strong? It was later that reality would hit Roger and his tears would come easily. After our prayer, the doctors left, and we were alone in a small gray room with the weight of the world on our shoulders.

"What are you thinking?" Roger asked.

"I want to change the channel. I don't like this program. Roger, I know God is with us, but I want to see evidence that he is right here, right now."

We prayed again that God would give us understanding, strength and reassurance to face the days ahead.

As we slowly walked back to Michael's room, I felt a struggle within me, a resistance, a desire to run away. Michael was facing weeks of pain and perhaps death.

How would he endure it? I thought.

Actually, that's not all that I was thinking. I was also thinking, *How could I endure it?* As I came face to face with my own selfishness, my heart forced me to look at the cross. If Jesus committed himself to endure the pain, the agony and suffering to see me freed from sin, I could make the same commitment to Michael to see him through anything. The decision was made. The hour had come to tell Michael.

A Bitter Pill

The remainder of the week was a flurry of medical tests—and tests of endurance. Michael's rigorous first day started with a bone marrow test. How do you explain a bone marrow test to a child, especially when he thought the doctor said "bow and arrow"? It took six people to hold him down when the doctor said, "Now, I'm drawing the 'target' on your back with brown soap." Looking into Michael's face, then glancing over his shoulder, I felt faint as I held tightly on to his arms.

His body jerked as they shoved a small pipe-like object into his hip bone and drew out the bone marrow. Anesthetics to relieve pain cannot reach into the bone marrow. What we couldn't know was that he would have more than forty of these grueling procedures in the course of the next three years.

The first oral medication that he was given was an extremely bitter cortisone pill. Nothing could mask its acrid taste. Besides the pill, he was given a powerful IV drug that would attack the leukemia cells, but would also cause extreme nausea.

Fortunately, we had been talking to Michael about the courage of King David. We had shared how God helped David face the things he feared. After six trips to the bathroom to vomit, Michael said, "Mom, I'm getting braver and braver."

Michael would have to take more than fifteen different types of oral medication over the course of the next three years. Unfortunately, the memory of that first bitter pill and the nausea was indelibly etched in his mind. The following three years brought a torturous, daily battle to get Michael to swallow his medicines. When a child realizes he cannot control what is happening to him, he tries to take control wherever he can. For Michael, it became his swallowing mechanism; that was one thing he thought he could control. His refusal to take medicine caused us to approach the matter firmly, creatively, sympathetically and forcefully and with all God's energy which so powerfully worked in us (Colossians 1:29). It was emotionally and physically exhausting. Our ultimate solution was to wake him in the night when he was too tired to fight. We hated the conflict as much as he did, but there was no choice: To live he had to keep up the daily medication.

Side Effects

Besides the frequent nausea, the chemotherapy he received that summer had pronounced side effects. His hair fell out, his body swelled and his muscles weakened. It was hard to believe this bloated little boy was the same child we had seen playing ball so vigorously only months before.

Thinking back, I remember bittersweet moments of seeing his courage, appreciating precious times together and feeling God's reassuring love. Other memories of Michael that first summer flood our minds—swinging a bat and falling down, clattering dishes at 5:00 a.m. because of a ferocious appetite caused by the medicine, and enduring the cruel reactions of other children who simply didn't understand.

One day Michael was playing at a nearby park while we watched our daughter, Christie, play softball. Soon he came to the car and sullenly sat down. After coaxing him to talk, we learned why he was so hurt. Several bigger boys had talked him into climbing up the slide. Then, as he slid down, they spit at him, threw rocks at him and called him names because of his appearance. *How could they treat him this way? Didn't they have any idea of what he was going through?* Of course they didn't. Again, my mind flashed back to the cross and I understood how the Father must have felt when Jesus said, "Father, forgive them for they know not what they do."

The cross was vivid again the day a spinal tap took six attempts...and another day when the scars on his back made a bone marrow test a longer, more painful ordeal...and still another day when the doctor had to probe Michael's veins to find a clear space to push the needle through. IV treatments, which had once been fairly simple, were now becoming rigorous, emotional ordeals. His veins began to collapse from overuse, bursting and burning his skin from the inside out. The cross was more real to us than ever. Watching our son suffer such agony put us more in touch with God's feelings as he had to watch his son, Jesus, suffer on the cross.

What Is Bad?

In our quest to gain our son's health, we discovered a new quest: to answer the question asked by so many: "Why do bad things happen to good people?" We first considered, "What is bad?" Michael's leukemia was bad. The pain of his treatments was bad. The cruelty of other kids was bad. But, from God's perspective, something that seems very bad to us isn't necessarily bad. God can work good out of any "bad" situation (Romans 8:28). Discipline, for example, seems bad at the time; later, however, we see that discipline produces good results (Hebrews 12:7-11). If God were to treat us as an overprotective, permissive parent, we would never have to face or deal with any problems, and we would stay weak-willed and immature.

As we watched Michael face painful bone marrow tests, spinal taps and chemotherapy, we realized that these painful experiences were necessary to bring healing to his body. In a greater way, God watched his Son suffer pain and anguish on the cross. The cross was a "bad" thing, but God brought the ultimate good out of it. He gives us the spiritual healing we desperately need. Jesus' loving and deliberate walk to the cross encourages us not to run away from our own crosses.

God is not an overbearing tyrant, but a caring Father. He always provides for our needs in ways we, alone, could never imagine. During our initial stay at the hospital, floods of calls came in from Christians everywhere. The most encouraging call was from Kip McKean, who had been the campus minister at our church in Charleston, Illinois, but was then in Boston as the lead evangelist. He called to tell us that Elena had given birth to their first child, Olivia, on Michael's sixth birthday, the same day that we had gotten his diagnosis. New life always gives hope. Today, when we see Olivia, we see living evidence of the years God has given life to Michael.

Christian brothers and sisters around the world prayed for Michael daily. Our precious church family in Charleston met needs before we realized we had them. They completely sterilized and redecorated Michael's room and planted flowers in front of our house.

Even the financial burden was obviously under God's control. Less than a week before we went to St. Louis Children's Hospital, my part-time job had offered full family health coverage at group rates to all employees, and we had signed up. Detail after detail was being taken care of by God.

People whose hearts had been hardened to the gospel were now softening. The church (and we personally) had just come through a period of intense persecution and criticism by our local newspaper. People who had believed the accusations had pulled away from us skeptically. But through this intense, personal tragedy, people began to view us with different eyes.

Would it take the death of a child to cause blind men to see? I wondered.

In God's case, it did; it took the painful and cruel death of his Son on a Roman cross.

Is God the author of bad things? The Bible teaches that every "good and perfect gift" comes from God (James 1:17). Paul's thorn in the flesh was a messenger of Satan (2 Corinthians 12:7). Satan is our enemy, but God is our "rescuer" (Colossians 1:13). Michael learned who the enemy was, yet it was hard for him to understand what was happening to him. Why was the cure so painful and sickening if it was supposed to be good?

That first summer he came to his own conclusion: "The good cells and the medicine are in Jesus' army. The bad cells are in the devil's army. There is a big war inside me, but Jesus' army will win." As grown-ups, we knew that God has the power to win, but the victory might come at the end of a shortened life as a home in heaven.

Watching Michael's physical battle helped me to understand our spiritual battles more clearly. 1 Peter 4:1 teaches us not to be surprised at the painful trials we suffer and to arm ourselves with the attitude of Christ. It took reliance on God for us to stay "clear minded and self-controlled" so that we could pray and not be overcome with doubts, fears and worries. We continued in our wholehearted service to God as a family.

In contrast, we observed that other families coping with having seriously ill children cut themselves off from other people and God, and simply fell apart. We later learned that a high percentage of marriages under this kind of pressure end in divorce. The inability to communicate keeps up walls that need to come down as two people go through their own grief. The need to blame something or someone for a child's illness gives an opening for blaming and attacking one another. While under pressure, the "cracks" in relationships show up. To undergo the intense pressure of a child's illness, people must draw on a strength beyond themselves. We turned to our "rescuer" daily, trusting that he would lift us up and make us strong (1 Peter 5:6-10). We longed for other families to have what we had and shared with as many as we could.

Asking the Questions

Still the question would linger: *Why? Why my child ? Why now?* One of the "whys" was answered for me in the song "This World Is Not My Home." Difficulties, hardships and illnesses remind me that there is a better life ahead of us. If this life were always perfect, we would get so caught up in it that we would never long to be in our perfect home with God. Children have a beautiful sense of heaven. When our neighbor's child died, our other son David (three years old at the time) expressed that he wished Shane hadn't died and gone to heaven yet. "I wanted Shane to wait for me," he said.

In addition to reminding us of our better home, bad things can be used to refine our character and faith. Paul says,

> ...we also rejoice in our sufferings because we know that suffering produces perseverance; perseverance, character; and character, hope. And hope does not disappoint us, because God has poured out his love into our hearts by the Holy Spirit, whom he has given us.
>
> *Romans 5:3-5*

Hope is a confident expectation. Through overcoming what

eventually became a three-year bout with leukemia, Michael's confidence and character have been greatly refined by God. After we moved to suburban Chicago, his fourth-grade teacher told me, "In a word, your son is wholesome." She admitted that at the beginning of school she had been concerned about his adjustment to a new city, new school, new friends and a new philosophy of teaching. Due to his illness and frequent isolation periods, Michael had missed a lot of his basics in education. His primary schooling experiences had been in an open classroom with independent studies, but his new school was as traditional as "reading, writing and arithmetic." Most children would have folded under the pressure, but Michael came back stronger. I ponder in my mother's heart what plan God has for Michael in his kingdom as a result of this experience.

Back to the haunting questions: *Why? Why this way?* The definitive answer comes as it came to Job. God answered Job by asking *him* a few questions. "Where were you when I laid the earth's foundation? Tell me, if you understand. Who marked off its dimensions? Surely you know!" (Job 38:4-5a). For two chapters, God quizzed Job about his understanding of the earthly creation.

> Job responded, "I am unworthy—how can I reply to you? I put my hand over my mouth. I spoke once but I have no answer—twice, but I will say no more"
>
> *Job 40:4-5*

Much as Job, we sometimes feel that God owes us an explanation, yet can we comprehend God's purpose and design of his natural world? Can we hope to comprehend how he deals with every aspect of our lives? When circumstances that we cannot control come into our lives, it helps us to see that we're not the big center of a small plan but a small part of a greater plan. Perhaps the circumstance is God's way to help people see their need for him. Perhaps it comes to teach our children, or the church or the lost. Who can really say? We may not understand all the "whys" of this life, or even all the "whys" of God's ways, but we can be thankful that we serve a God who says, "My grace is sufficient for you, for my power is made perfect in weakness" (2 Corinthians 12:9).

In our weakest moments, God's power is always made known and his promises always hold truth. During the seven months that Michael's IV treatments became more arduous due to his collapsed veins, I kept holding on to God's promises. The one I held on to the most tightly was that "God will not let you be tempted beyond what you can bear" (1 Corinthians 10:13b). I had some heart-to-heart prayers with God about this. "Father, I know changing a few cells in a little boy's body would be no task for you. You know whether or not Michael is cured right now. If he is, Father, could you please just let the doctor know so he can get Michael off this stuff? I feel like I am coming close to the 'more than I can bear' limit, and so is Michael." Within the week our doctor said, "I think Michael has taken about all he can handle. Let's see if we can take him off chemotherapy early."

After going through some final tests, Michael was taken off his medication completely! Today, his life is a joy to so many people: his doctors, his parents, his grandparents, his brother and sister, and also to all the Christians who so faithfully prayed on his behalf all over the world.

We learned above all that if you know God, you can truly rejoice in your sufferings. Bad things are from the devil. Yet God can make good come from even that. His grace is sufficient. His Son has shown us. Yet, if the story had ended differently, if Michael had died, we could have still rejoiced, because Michael would have reached his goal—a home with God in heaven. No matter how difficult the circumstances, he never puts us in a no-win position.

We serve a great God!

2

Bad Things Keep Happening

Consider it pure joy, my brothers, whenever you face trials of many kinds, because you know that the testing of your faith develops perseverance. Perseverance must finish its work so that you may be mature and complete, not lacking anything.

James 1:2-4

Ten years ago, I wrote the chapter you just read. I wanted that chapter to end, "and they lived happily ever after." But...it didn't! Michael did survive; that is the good news. Yet, the bad news is that "bad" things kept happening to our family. If I were not the one living this life, I would wonder if it were fiction.

On a cold January morning in 1987, I put my husband, Roger, on a plane to Germany. He was going to discuss the possibility of beginning a new church in Munich, Germany. As a young man, Roger had graduated from an American high school in Germany. Later, as a young married couple, we made extensive plans to go to Germany to build a church and start a Christian school there. That door was soon shut, but another one opened: Roger was offered an opportunity to preach for a small church on the edge of a university campus in Charleston, Illinois. But, through the years, beginning a new church in Germany was a dream that had continued to live in Roger's heart.

One memory from his high school days in Germany was particularly vivid to Roger. As a high school senior in 1965, he had visited the Berlin Wall with some of his friends. Its austerity and the forbidden fortress of barbed wire and land mines were a curiosity to the group of boys who playfully hoisted each other up the West Berlin side to take souvenirs from the top of the wall. When it was Roger's turn to scale the wall, his eye caught the eye of a woman gazing back at him from the other side. She was watching him and his friends enjoying their freedom when suddenly he became aware of rifles protruding through slits in bricked-up windows. The seriousness of a city divided sobered him and stayed with him for many years. So it seemed that in 1987, God was actually granting Roger's life-long dream to see the kingdom flourish in Germany.

Just as over the years many have tested the strength of that dividing wall, God was about to test the strength of our hearts.

Could It Be Happening Again?

At this point, Michael had been in remission from leukemia for more than five years and free of chemotherapy for three years. A rough-and-tumble eleven-year-old, he had been officially pronounced cured of leukemia in 1986. A week before Roger left for Germany, Michael suffered a serious concussion playing keep-away at a New Year's Eve party in Chicago. We ended up celebrating the new year in the emergency room of a busy Chicago hospital. When Michael seemed to be recovering, the doctors sent him home after a few days of observation.

The day I put Roger on the plane, everyone involved felt confident that within the next few days Michael would have fully recuperated. But, by that evening Michael became violently ill, so ill that his oncologist feared the worst—Michael might be experiencing a relapse of leukemia. The only way to be sure was to put him through a series of tests again. We had seen other heartbroken families endure relapse after relapse. The thought of facing another three years of chemotherapy, bone marrow procedures and spinal taps seemed horrifying.

Can we possibly go through this again? I lamented in my heart.

Michael was braver than I was at that moment. I felt very alone without Roger's strength, but the childlike faith of our son helped me to be strong.

"I guess God knows that we can do this without Dad or he wouldn't have let him fly to Germany," he said. "Besides, he is doing an important thing for God. You don't need to have Dad come back unless it's...you know...cancer."

The next day a battery of tests were scheduled. Christie, David, Michael and I all prayed together for the tests to go well.

Later, I slipped off alone to pray to God for strength. Pouring out my true feelings, I identified the source of much of my anxiety: I was afraid that what was happening to Michael was God's answer to a prayer Roger and I had prayed when Michael first got sick. We had prayed, "If Michael is *not* going to be a faithful disciple when he grows up, take him to heaven as an innocent child." I shared my anguish with God and prayed that I would feel his strength through the next few days.

As I continued to pray, I remembered a sermon that I had heard on changing God's mind. On a few occasions, prophets had changed God's mind about destroying the sinful Israelites. One plea stuck with me: Moses prayed that God would not destroy his people in order to spare his reputation as a faithful God:

> "If you put these people to death all at one time, the nations who have heard this report about you will say, 'The LORD was not able to bring these people into the land he promised them on oath; so he slaughtered them in the desert.'"
>
> *Numbers 14:15-16*

In our situation God's reputation was also on the line. People from all over the world had consistently prayed for Michael's cure. What would his relapse or his death do to their faith in God? God would be totally open to misrepresentation again by man's faithless view of him. For the first time, I felt more concern for God's reputation than for my own pain. I came away from that prayer time with a deeper respect for God and deeper desire to give him the glory that he deserves.

Waiting for Test Results

By this time, Michael was extremely weak from vomiting and fighting relentless pain. We had to haul him from test to test in a little hospital wagon. Two close friends, Chris Fuqua and Roger Parlour came to help. I was so grateful they were there to support me. As it turned out, it took all three of us to hold Michael absolutely still for the crucial forty-five minute spinal tap. A needle assembly was inserted and left in his spine while the doctors tested the spinal fluid for cancerous cells. In the event that the fluid did contain cancerous cells, the doctors would then have the immediate access necessary to inject drugs directly into his spinal fluid. Michael begged us to let him move. His legs cramped and his feet tingled. Sweat poured out of every pore as if he were running a race for his life. Any movement would have caused serious injury to his spine. Those agonizing minutes gave me a taste of how God must have felt watching his son writhe on the cross for six hours.

After more tests and a CAT scan, we waited for what seemed like an eternity for the doctor's results.

To God's glory, the top specialist in the field of spinal health was holding a symposium at Chicago Children's Hospital that very day. Our doctor asked him to look at Michael's test results. The verdict—no leukemia! All the trauma was a direct result of the concussion he had received on New Year's Eve. Exhausted from the day's events, Michael and I cried and held each other as we made the happy phone call to Germany to tell Dad that everything was all right and he wouldn't need to rush home. Within a few days, Michael was even playing basketball again!

I had never felt so close to God as I did during those few days—days when I had to totally rely on his strength because mine had failed me and my husband was not physically with me. It was then that I made the promise to God that I would write a book about our experiences to help other families. Roger came home not only to a physically healthy son but to a more spiritually healthy wife.

3

Ready, Willing, but Not Able

The Lord is not slow in keeping his promise, as some understand slowness. He is patient with you, not wanting anyone to perish, but everyone to come to repentance.

2 Peter 3:9

Life with God is an ongoing growing process. I learn something; then I either relearn it or find a new way to apply it. At the same time God teaches me new things. In short, God is patient with us as his people. He is faithful to keep teaching us if we just stay determined to trust him and hold on to him no matter what.

In the late '70s, Roger and I were involved in the forerunning of God's modern-day spiritual movement. I sincerely believe that God simply used what he had to work with at the time. He started little, but he started powerfully, using every weak vessel who was willing to be used. The movement started in Boston in 1979 with thirty people who were committed to be disciples and to keep that as a standard for every member of the church. The Boston church has planted other churches that have planted other churches in all the major cities of the world. The movement has grown to encompass the globe with disciples everywhere.

We found that while God was using us to spread the gospel the best we knew how, he was also refining our character and faith. During this time, God allowed me to go through many trials with my health, allowing me often to function only in "first gear." I knew he wanted me to learn to rely on him, and possibly he wanted me to write about it some day, helping others to stay faithful during their difficult times.

A Decision to Be Ready

Let me backtrack a little to give you perspective on my life. Don't worry—I won't go back to "when I was a little girl." I will go back to the time I decided to choose to be sane. The children were small and our family life was out of control, mainly because I could barely figure out what I was supposed to do each day in order to take care of three little children and a husband and a neurotic dog. Roger was preparing to go out of town for a week-long meeting. Two of the children and I had been stung by a nest of yellow jackets the previous week. Out of that experience, I discovered that I was allergic to bee and wasp stings. My paranoia got so bad that one night I pulled all the flowers out of the flower bed in front of our house because I knew that the yellow jackets were going to kill me. I was sure that they purposely stayed by our front door to torment me. I was in a panic about Roger's upcoming trip because I was also sure that if he left, I would get stung and die alone with three little kids.

I was just about to lose it emotionally. Roger talked me through my fears enough to help me realize that my greatest fear was that I would die and go to hell. I wasn't sure if my life matched up to the Bible's definition of a true follower of Christ. We talked, prayed and studied the Bible together until I felt assurance that God would help me resolve my fears. I remember specifically considering whether to go ahead and flip out and let other people take over my life and my children or to stay sane. I thought about Jesus' decision to die for me. My decision to live for him every day, as full of faith and as sane as possible, felt as daunting to me as his decision to die. My walk with God became literally a moment-by-moment act of faith.

Time passed and I began to feel more confident about life. I thought, "Okay, God, thank you very much, you have been a big help to me, but I'm pretty grown up now, so I think I can handle things on my own. I appreciate it." It was then that Michael got leukemia. Time to go back to kindergarten!

More "Bad Things"

Although God had blessed us incredibly during the leukemia years, I was exhausted at the end of the time. Added stress came with chronic lack of sleep and with the weighty responsibilities of leading the women's ministry. I had come from a church background where the minister's wife was not necessarily involved with the day-to-day ministry to the congregation. The concept was, "He does the ministry; I do the kids and the house." Now that Roger and I were part of the cutting edge of a movement that called for total commitment and total involvement from every member, I had much adjusting to do. As a couple we were to actually lead the ministry together, with me leading the women.

My own mental and physical health was deteriorating. Spiritually, I had highs but progressively more lows. Roger's ministry responsibilities were increasing as my abilities to lead were decreasing. To see his wife being depressed when God had blessed us with Michael's cure and with so much great spiritual input, frustrated and confused him. He felt helpless to help me. I felt helpless to help myself. The depression deepened and continued.

More and more I was physically and emotionally able to do less and less. Migraine headaches became a weekly event. Also, I did not realize for several years that I was hypoglycemic, which caused me frequently to be taken home from meetings and appointments due to weakness and cold shakes. I was also getting weaker because my periods were almost to the point of hemorrhaging and lasted three weeks at a time. Besides the migraines, I would have intense body pains that made rolling over in bed excruciatingly painful. But I was the minister's wife, and I had duties to perform with grace and dignity. I could not allow myself to fall prey to my own body and emotions—that would not be a good example—so I trudged to meetings in an almost incoherent state, causing people to wonder about the condition of my faith and my commitment. Roger's frustration and my depression (and low self-esteem) seemed about to take me down.

In 1985 I was warned by a doctor that one of my pap smears came back showing precancerous cells. In 1986 I consulted several doctors about what course of action to take and got conflicting advice. Finally one doctor did a suctioning of the lining of my uterus and scheduled me for a hysterectomy on the basis of precancerous cells that he found. The surgery was scheduled for Christmas. Also at this time, our ministry insurance switched to an HMO, a plan with greater coverage for less money. This was a great blessing since we had been paying monthly premiums of over $600.00. (Our insurance premiums had skyrocketed because of Michael's leukemia. Because of his preexisting illness, we could not make an independent decision to switch companies. Since we certainly needed coverage for him, we were stuck with the company.)

Unfortunately, I turned out to be a financial detriment to the budget for the HMO, and the hysterectomy, under yet another doctor, was canceled. I was told that their lab did not see any bad cells on the slide. (Ironically, after my cancer surgery, the slide and any record of it had disappeared.) For the next nine months I endured pain, migraines and bleeding that seemed to be getting worse and worse. More biopsies were taken, and still nothing showed up. I begged my gynecologist to do something, and he finally gave me progesterone, which is the hormone that counteracts estrogen. I had been praying that God would please oversee my care and move the doctors to do the right things for my life.

Months later we would learn that God *had* intervened. The hormone progesterone probably prolonged my life because the type cancer we were to find that I had, feeds on estrogen. The progesterone served to temporarily starve the cancer.

Spiritual Pain

The trauma of any critical illness is a true assault on a person's total being. My personal battle with illness came at a time when I was going through some deep soul-searching battles. I had lived for years with the gnawing thought that my relationship with God was not right. Even though my husband and I had been in the ministry for many years, I did not feel the confidence in my salvation that the Bible promises: "I write these things to you who believe in the name of the Son of God so that you may know that you have eternal life" (1 John 5:13). The confident knowledge that is repeated over and over in the book of 1 John was not in my heart. In fact, what was in my heart was a constant condemnation.

John tells us that sometimes our hearts will condemn us without just cause, but God is "greater than our hearts, and he knows everything" (1 John 3:19-20). Knowing that I tend to be a self-condemning person by nature, I needed guidance in knowing whether I was experiencing conviction from God or condemnation from my own deceptive heart. I had to get to the bottom of this dilemma because it was undermining my ability to help other people. I prayed constantly for God to help me resolve my unsettled heart as well as fix my rebellious body.

At a leadership conference in Boston, Massachusetts, in August of 1987, God gave me a rare and wonderful opportunity to be with all the women who had had a significant spiritual impact on my life. I got with each one of them and asked them to tell me their overview of my spiritual life and relationship with God. It was as if God had orchestrated this event to help me retrace the spiritual steps I had taken over the past fifteen years. I fasted and prayed that God would help me to resolve my doubts.

Having been a religious, moral person who had tried to follow the Bible most of my life, I did not experience a dramatic turning point like those who repent of adultery or drunkenness. But God began to reveal my self-righteous heart. I had worked hard to win God's approval, but it was all my "good deeds" that I was banking on to save me. I needed to understand the unconditional love of God and the power of salvation found at the cross and the cross only (Romans 1:16-17; 1 Corinthians 15:1-2). My Christian walk had been very performance-oriented because my initial "conversion" was very works-oriented. I ran down the list of things to do to be saved and checked them off, including baptism by immersion. I had put my faith in my obedience rather than in what Jesus did for me on the cross.

Why do bad things keep happening to "good" people? Well, this "good" person needed to learn that only God is good and only God can make us good through the sacrifice of Jesus. I had become an excellent Pharisee, but I had not become a disciple. I had obeyed the letter of the law, but my heart was not humble before God. It was years after my initial immersion that I began to hear lessons on being a disciple. The passage in Matthew 28:18-20 bothered me because it said that the apostles were to go make disciples and baptize them. I was baptized and then later learned what a disciple was. I had not been "born again"; I had been "stillborn."

After that long weekend in August, I resolved first to be certain that I was committed to being a true disciple of Jesus. How thankful I am that God knew I had a heart that was willing to follow him and repent. Then, as a disciple, I was baptized by faith in God's power to save me and enable me to change.

I praise God that, through the years, even when I was going through confusing times physically, spiritually and emotionally, he continued to use me and my family to advance his kingdom—as only God can do. He made me ready, willing and *finally* able.

4

This Doesn't Feel Like Love

"'Has God forgotten to be merciful?
    Has he in anger withheld his compassion?"

Selah

Then I thought, "To this I will appeal:
    the years of the right hand of the Most High."
I will remember the deeds of the LORD;
    yes, I will remember your miracles of long ago.
I will meditate on all your works
    and consider all your mighty deeds.

Psalm 77: 9-12

"Mrs. Lamb, the news is worse than we first thought. You actually have two types of cancer. One is leiomyosarcoma, which is found in the lining of the uterus. It is rare and usually strikes women in their 70s. It is a very aggressive cancer. You also have a cancerous tumor within your uterus. And I'm afraid that we have detected some cancer cells outside the uterine wall."

I will never forget those words spoken to me in October of 1987. How confusing they were to someone who more than ever had put her trust in God. Why would God let this happen to one of his children whom he loved? This sure didn't feel like love.

The Diagnosis

I was in downtown Chicago finalizing visas for Roger and me to travel. We were planning to fly to Sydney, Bombay and Johannesburg to speak and to encourage the new churches there. To my dismay, I began to hemorrhage badly. After two days of intense bleeding, I would be ignored no longer! When the doctor said that he *might* be able to do an emergency surgical procedure to diagnose the problem at 7:00 a.m. the following morning, I said, "I'll be there!" At 11:00 p.m. the next day it was finally done.

A day of no eating or drinking while waiting for an open surgery slot gave me a deeper appreciation of how Jesus must have felt in the desert and the night before Calvary.

It took a few days before the report came back, so feeling much better physically, I proceeded with my plans to speak at a Christian women's conference in downstate Illinois that weekend. It was Friday morning at the busy Midway airport. Roger and I were thankful for the time to wait for my flight and reflect on the previous week's events. There he was again, my tower of strength, encouraging me with his confident smile, and his blue eyes giving me "The Look" which meant that everything would be all right.

Knowing that the lab results of the surgery would be ready that morning, we discussed whether to call before I left to speak or wait till I came home Saturday night. If it were good news and I waited till Saturday to find out, I would miss the opportunity to share my joy. Not knowing might also open me up to a weekend of anxiety and dread. If the news were bad..."Well, it just would not be bad news," I reasoned.

Calling the doctor on a pay phone gave me an eerie sense of *deja vu*. Years ago I had called a doctor on a pay phone eagerly anticipating the results of a pregnancy test. That phone call had thrilled me with the news, "Yes! You are pregnant!" Nine months later our first baby, Christie, was born.

For different reasons, this time also my fingers shook and trembled to hit the right buttons. The pit in my stomach jumped up to my throat as I choked out the words, "Did you get the results of my lab tests yet?"

"Yes, Mrs. Lamb. We did detect cancer, and you will need to be scheduled for surgery Monday morning," said the doctor.

Unable to take in the shock of the news, I said, "Can't it wait a few months? My husband and I have speaking engagements in India and South Africa in a few weeks."

"No, Mrs. Lamb, it cannot wait. You will have to cancel your plans and come in Monday morning at 7:00 a.m."

As if on automatic pilot, I said, "Can I go to Peoria this weekend?" (I think it was Peoria. I honestly have forgotten where I went. If any readers remember that weekend, please let me know!)

"You can do whatever you like until Monday morning," he said. "Good-bye."

Still dazed, I told Roger, "He said I could go to Peoria, but I cannot go to South Africa or India."

During the next few minutes he asked me a thousand questions to which I had no answers. I felt as if I were in a foggy land in another dimension for hours.

"You will stay home, and I'll call the women in charge to cancel for you," said Roger.

"Oh, that won't be necessary," I said, "They just *think* it is cancer. They won't know till they do the surgery. I'll be fine. Besides, I think I need to be at this conference to get prepared spiritually. Chris Fuqua will be there and Pat Gempel and all my friends from Charleston and Champaign. I think I need to be with them right now."

Hopeful that it really was not cancer, Roger prayed with me and sent me off.

Still in denial, I am sure that I must have downplayed the results of the lab tests to everyone. It was an encouraging time to be with my soul-mate sisters. The only thing I remember about my speech is that it was totally from God. I was so tired and nervous before I got up to speak that Chris Fuqua had to pull me aside, pray and encourage me to trust God. I shared with deep conviction that everyone must be serious about getting right with God.

Then, during my speech, I finally came to grips with the truth of the doctor's report. I shared the news with the women, and asked them to pray for me. I was ready to get back home and face the next few days with renewed strength.

That Saturday night, Roger and I went away alone for a precious romantic evening. We treasured our time together as if it were going to be our last. Not knowing what was ahead, we felt the need to make special memories.

Sunday I was encouraged both at worship with my church family and in prayer with my physical family. I needed the spiritual boost.

Monday morning arrived. I felt ready. The elders and ministers were there to pray for me and anoint me with oil (James 5:14).

Surgery and Radiation

The nurses came to take me to surgery. The cold room was prepared and waiting for me. The doctors took their places under the spotlight. One of the surgeons was trying to get a laugh when he said that the guys in the lab couldn't wait to get ahold of my uterus (because my cancer was so rare). It was a bad joke, so I was grateful to drift off to sleep.

The radical hysterectomy, hospital stay and flurry of doctors' visits are a blur in my memory. After my surgery, what I *do* vividly remember are nights of intense pain, keeping me awake for hours—pain from the incision and abdominal adjustments. The only comfortable position was a prayerful kneeling one. I found God's reminder a bit humorous and obvious; I needed to be praying. I was struggling with believing that God truly loved me since he was allowing me to go through such a torturous ordeal. The doubt about his compassion for me was more hurtful than my actual physical pain.

For the next seven weeks I went through daily abdominal radiation treatments. Radiation therapy feels like being sunburned from the inside out. It was so painful I was illogically tempted to swallow sun screen to protect the inflamed lining of my organs, but I knew that would be futile since my frequent trips to the bathroom eliminated anything and everything that entered that tender territory.

Lying still and silent on the radiation table gave me too much time to think. I kept replaying old science fiction movies in my head as the shell-like machine encircled my body. The sound of its whirring and clanging echoed off the cold, sterile walls. My nurse became a "Mad Scientist," and at times I wanted to attack her for what she was doing to my body.

Some of the exams and treatments were too humiliating for me even to mention here. It seemed that my body suddenly became part of a lab experiment that medical science had a right to conduct as inhumanely as possible. But God's presence and Jesus' example of giving to others, while impaled and humiliated on his cross, forced me to keep still and to keep a spiritual mindset. For the first time in my life I felt that I could relate to some of what Jesus felt on the cross as people gawked at his body hanging on painful display.

I encountered doctors and nurses with varying degrees of sensitivity. The most harsh of the doctors came in as a consult toward the end of my radiation treatments. By this time, touching anything below my belly button caused raw pain. This particular doctor did not seem to realize this. His callous manner reminded me of little boys who liked to tear the legs off of grasshoppers. I could not help screaming in pain and crying, which seemed to annoy him. After feeling assaulted by a few bad experiences, I had Roger go to the exams with me for emotional and physical support.

Another doctor had the bedside manner of a corpse. I think maybe he breathed too much formaldehyde working on the cadavers in medical school.

My experience with these doctors would later cause me to greatly appreciate the doctor who followed up my case in Boston, Dr. Robert McClellan. He was an answer to prayer. He greeted me as if it were a privilege for him to be treating me. "People like you are why we go to medical school," he would say. He was especially sensitive to my emotional and physical state.

Observing our shock at his demeanor, he told us the secret behind his compassion. During medical school, one of the male students was sent into an examining room and put up in stirrups just as his women patients would be. The room was darkened, the examining light was turned on and the class passed by, looking at him with his legs spread apart. The head doctor then said, "I don't want any of you ever to forget how you felt today. Treat your patients with dignity."

Physical and Emotional Weakness

As the radiation attacked all the fast-growing cells in my body (good and bad), my body's strength was focused on healing the besieged areas. Therefore, my energy was drained, leaving me in an incredibly weakened state.

My recuperation went something like this: Get up and eat, lay down exhausted, shower, lay down exhausted, spend an hour in the bathroom eliminating breakfast, get dressed, lay down exhausted, ride to the hospital for radiation treatments, get treatment, maybe eat, sleep all the way home, sleep till supper, eat, lay down exhausted, spend an hour in the bathroom eliminating lunch and dinner, go to bed exhausted.

At the same time, my emotional strength also weakened because of the radical surgery and the subsequent hormone depletion. I had to continue taking progesterone, which suppressed my body's estrogen level. I had no more "happy hormones" left. I had gone through years of premenstrual syndrome (PMS) earlier—humorously referred to as "Persecute My Spouse"—but this time there was no relief. Because of the estrogen depletion, I was left with no "up" times—only "down" times! I literally felt as though I had PMS continuously, day after day, for what would ultimately be six long years. I became depressed both emotionally and spiritually.

At my lowest point I remember thinking, "God! I thought that you were supposed to love me. This certainly does not feel like love." I still had much to learn about God and the sureness of his love.

5

Out of the Mire

I waited patiently for the LORD;
    he turned to me and heard my cry.
He lifted me out of the slimy pit,
    out of the mud and mire;
he set my feet on a rock
    and gave me a firm place to stand.

Psalm 40:1-2

Why should God love you? Look at you. What good are you to him now? God's not happy with you. This is the punishment that you've deserved throughout your life. He's trying to get rid of you so he can get Roger a better wife—a wife who can keep up with him and be strong for the ministry.

Confused by the message that my cancer diagnosis was sending me, I became an easy target for Satan's attacks. I had finally put my confidence in God for my salvation, and now two months later I was told that I might die. I was nearly certain that it was a sign from God that he was fed up with me and ready to rid the earth of me.

At least God was gracious enough to wait till I got my relationship with him right, I thought. *But, God, is this any way to treat a sick woman? It sure doesn't feel like love.*

I was tormented every day with these thoughts, finally collapsing in an emotional heap. I felt guilty because I knew my thinking was wrong, and allowing Satan to win was certainly wrong. I was in the ministry. I was leading people. How could I even think thoughts like this? How could I let Satan win like this? I knew I had to fight, but how? My loving husband's arms could not heal this pain or shield me from these thoughts. I knew I needed God. I pored through the Bible trying to find answers.

Two Questions

I had fought for my faith before when Michael was diagnosed with leukemia. At that time I had faith that God's love for an innocent child was a certainty. But now I was not so certain about his love for me as an adult—a sinful adult who had surely disappointed him often. Understanding that questioning God's love was the sinful, faithless root that had to be cut out of my heart, I resolved that these doubts would be crucified forever.

I searched for the answer to two specific questions: (1) How do I know that God loves me? and (2) Do I love him? My study and soul-searching brought the following insights during that difficult time:

How Do I Know That God Loves Me?

The answer is as profound as it is simple: John 3:16 says, "For God so loved the world that he gave his one and only Son." What more do I need from God to prove that he loves me? In Luke 11:29-30, Jesus rebuked the wicked crowd for always seeking a miraculous sign. He told them the only sign they needed was the sign of Jonah. An infinitely stronger sign was Jesus, buried in the belly of the earth for three days and raised to life. The only sign of God's love I need to see and understand is the cross and the empty tomb. What further proof of God's love do I need?

It appalls me that I demand more proof. It's like I'm heartlessly thinking: *Okay, so you let your only Son die for me. So what, I need more! A promise of getting to heaven—well, that's not enough for me!* Think again, Marcia! Getting an opportunity to repent, be forgiven and go to heaven is *all* I need; the rest is like icing on the cake.[1]

Do I Love God?

Do I have to look at this side of it? Well, since any relationship is two-sided, yes I do. When I examine my own heart, it is evident that my love for God is so conditional. When things go well, I love him. When things go bad, I'm not sure I even like him. How fickle! When he is answering prayers the way I like—prayers about health, financial security, marital bliss, harmonious relationships, successful children and a fruitful ministry, then I really love him.

But when hard times hit, so do my doubts. I have more of a commitment to my husband, even with his imperfections, than I do to my perfect God. Somehow, I have the idea that God is supposed to just make me happy and grant all my wishes. Instead of "my Father who art in heaven," it's more like "my genie who art in the lamp." Too often I think, *It is his job to make me happy.*

When I realize just how sinful my attitude toward God is at times, it truly humbles me. 1 Peter 5:6 comes to life, "Humble yourselves, therefore, under God's mighty hand, that he may lift you up in due time." God has had his mighty hand on me for a long time. He needed to get my attention long enough for me to stop and examine him and his great love for me— long enough for me to repent of my pitiful and ungrateful attitudes toward him.

I became determined to be content with the knowledge of God's forgiveness and the ultimate proof of his love through Jesus...whether or not I ever saw another blessing in my life. In spite of my sinful heart, he continued to bless me more than I could ask or imagine. That's the God who loves me and loves all of us—beyond a shadow of a doubt (Romans 5:6-11).

The Cost of the Cure

Many friends prayed faithfully for my healing, and mercifully, when the radiation therapy finally ended, my cancer seemed to be arrested, but not all the physical challenges.

When our family moved to Boston, Massachusetts, in 1988, God was preparing the road to another healing process.

After two years of working in the ministry, including beginning a ministry to artists and musicians, it became evident that I was not able to physically keep up with the demands of the full-time work. Roger moved into the role of writer and editor of *UpsideDown Magazine*, and I took time off to recuperate and look for part-time work.

Although the probability of a cure certainly left me relieved, I wish I could say that gratitude overwhelmed me, but that wouldn't be the truth.

I began to see, with the help of friends like Gordon and Theresa Ferguson and Al and Gloria Baird, that I was angry with God. Yes, my life had been spared, and I should have been very grateful, but instead, I focused on the side effects of the cure. Along with needing to leave the full-time ministry, I continued to suffer pain from the internal intestinal alterations. Sexual intercourse with my husband became a searing, painful event, and my emotional state was at an all-time low. I wondered if I would ever be able to enjoy sex again and whether I would ever feel happy again. I had taken a deeper, darker plunge into a depression out of which I could be not be encouraged or will my way.

The fact is that cures often come at a great cost. Our salvation, our soul's cure, came at the cost of Jesus' suffering and death. Even Michael's leukemia cure came with costs to his health later as a teen (see Chapter 7). But when I focused on the cost, I missed the joy of the blessing and the opportunity to grow "through suffering according to God's will" (1 Peter 4:12-19; Romans 5:3-5). Focusing on the cost also suppressed my faith, which is vital to allow God to do his work.

Depression, my constant companion, gave me a reason to desperately rely on God's Spirit. I began to see the tools God had given me to combat my "thorn in the flesh." In my natural physical state, I was depleted of the elements that our bodies provide to "oil the gears" of pleasantness. I had to rely solely on God and his power; a happy or good mood would never carry me through a day. In my sinful nature, with or without estrogen, I had to admit that there was "no good thing in me." But as a disciple, God, and God alone, would produce in me the fruits of the Spirit: "love, joy, peace, patience, kindness, goodness, faithfulness and self-control" (Galatians 5:22-23).

I realized, in short, *how desperately* we all need to rely on God's Spirit to be spiritual and godly (Romans 8:5-11). I finally got the point: In my flesh, I am spiritually challenged. I have a Spirit-dependency. I learned that I must get up daily and decide to rely on God's Spirit to serve and love others.

Relying on "happy hormones" was not the avenue to a spiritual life, whether I had them or didn't have them.

God calls us to live one day at a time. My great friend, Sheila Jones, often reminds me: "Have enough faith for today, and if that's too difficult, then have enough faith for right now."

I have often heard my husband say, "We have the choice (1) to live by *our* spirit or (2) to die to ourselves and live by God's Spirit. Whose spirit do you think is more fun?"

The times I feel especially depleted of faith and joy, God provides encouragement from disciples like Sheila, my husband and my family, whose faith and hope I borrow again and again.

The Kiln of Faith

It would be years before I could look back on my pilgrimage and understand what lesson God was teaching me at this point in my life. The illustration of clay being molded and shaped by the potter was a recurring theme that offered some perspective on life to me. In the early days of my married life, I had molded my own life and gotten hardened by religious pride and sin. God had to break me and rework me until I was pliable to his molding and shaping me to become a true disciple of Jesus. After becoming a true disciple and being baptized, I needed to continue to learn to obey (Matthew 28:18-19). His re-creation of my life was then put into the kiln of faith. I needed to go through a refining fire that would set my faith and heart on God, that would cause me to trust him for my life and my salvation for eternity, no matter what happened.[2]

As I share my journey after becoming a disciple and what I have learned from it, there is something I want to make very clear. It is very painful for me to share. However, without sharing it, I will be unfair to many readers who have suffered in a similar way.

Some readers may have already concluded this from what I have written so far, but I now understand that for at least the prior twenty-five years of my life, I had been suffering from clinical depression and a host of related symptoms. But I thank God that I can share this part of my life from a point of victory. God has worked powerfully through a most challenging trial. It is almost too funny to think about all the incredible ways that God has used me in spite of this.[3]

Most of my "symptoms" surfaced after Christie was born. Much to Roger's dismay, the sweet, fun-loving wife that he had married, turned into a paranoid, edgy mess of emotion. Childbirth and initial motherhood is a scary time for all women—hormonal upheaval, lack of sleep, and the responsibility of feeding and taking care of a little nonreturnable lifeform. Feelings of guilt and disillusionment can be engulfing as women try to remember why motherhood was going to be such an awe-inspiring experience.

I was given medication to sleep for Christie's delivery, and that was the last good sleep I had for the next twenty-plus years. I did not sleep through the night without waking at least three times. Years of wakeful babies, Michael's bout with leukemia, followed by my own nightly body pains and panic attacks, kept waking me up, which added up to about twenty-five years of postpartum blues.

I was plagued by a crowd of opinionated demons (much more than the normal "mind clatter" that many people experience). Bombarded by these negative voices and by constant accusations, I held tightly to two favorite scriptures throughout years of these mental battles:

"...on this rock [the confession that Jesus is Lord] I will build my church, and the gates of Hades will not overcome it."
Matthew 16:18

The God of peace will soon crush Satan under your feet.
Romans 16:20

If you walked by my house and listened carefully, you could also hear me quote in a loud voice, "Get behind me, Satan!!" or "Peace! Be still!" I would sing songs such as "Peace, Perfect Peace" to quiet the panic attacks I experienced at night.

I was frustrated trying to think and make decisions in this dazed state of mental confusion. Growing weary in the daily battle to fight depression and the struggle to be happy, I begged God for solutions to what seemed to be a dismal future. I suspected the medication that was supposed to prolong my life was the cause of this latest overwhelming depression. *If this is what life will always be, I don't know if I want to prolong it,* I thought. I feared that my teenage children's memories of their mother would be dreadful. I knew that I was unreliable with a memory as short as...now what was I saying? After 8:00 p.m., I lived in a zombie state. Late night conversation melted into a slurring drone much like the adults' voices in "Peanuts" cartoons ("wah, wha, wah, wha, wah, waaaaaa").

God came to my rescue again! I talked to a close friend and Christian psychologist, Hardy Tillman, and he began to put the pieces of the puzzle together. Was I suffering from Post Traumatic Depression? Was the medication to suppress my estrogen the culprit? Was it unresolved guilt or sin, or was I experiencing mid-life crisis? In time we came to realize that it was none of the above! I was genuinely, clinically and chemically depressed. I was so happy to hear it!

Like a diabetic needs insulin, my brain was in dire need of a neurotransmitting chemical. The diagnosis was confirmed as I began to feel "normal" within a short amount of time of taking the chemical replacement. I was told that the medicine would not help me if I did not need it. I immediately had compassion on others who should be taking similar medication but are too ashamed or too "shamed" to do so.

Now I could think all the way through a full sentence. I could remember why I went to the store and even remember to bring home what I bought! A whole new world of memory and mental sharpness opened up to me. Decisions, any size decisions, were no longer a life-threatening experience for me.

To this day I do not understand how my incredible husband, Roger, could live with all my craziness. But to quote him, he says, "I love a challenge!"

Trained by God

The relief I experienced was welcomed, but please hear me clearly at this point. This for me is *the* heart of this book. I believe in "due time" God lifted me up (1 Peter 5:6), but I can now look back and be thankful for all that I learned before the relief came. If I had found quick easy answers to some of these challenges, I might never have sought God. But, because I looked at everything as a spiritual battle, I believe God trained me in ways that I would never have tolerated on my own. I would not have known the power of prayer. I would not have known that the Bible teaches that you can *learn* to love your husband and children—even when you don't feel like it (Titus 2:4-5). (And my husband and children might not have learned some lessons about loving me unconditionally.) I would not have learned to rely on God to make up for my weaknesses. I would not have known the incredible unconditional love of God. I would not have learned most of the lessons that I will share later in this book as we examine the Beatitudes and the power they unlock in our lives. I would have just popped another pill when things got rough.

An in-depth look at depression is beyond the scope of this book. However, it should be noted that depression can come from several sources. Some depression is a result of sin and when sin is dealt with, the depression lifts (see Psalm 32 and 38). Confession of sin to one another is often a powerful element in setting someone free. But if we think all depressed people just need to be told to repent, we are wrong.

Other forms of depression are relieved through counseling and through the presence of unconditional love. Many people will make great progress as someone helps them sort out various issues in their lives and loves them consistently.

But then some forms of depression clearly seem to be physically based. While many in society may be too quick to try to medicate away problems, prescription medication may help a person to return to normal. In my case, it has proved most helpful. No one should be ashamed of getting this kind of help, and we should not be hesitant to encourage people who are hurting to get it.

Of course, depression may have connections with all of the things I have mentioned, and the best help may come through a two- or three-pronged approach.

But what about those cases where there is no obvious cause and no obvious solution? (I know some who had hopes of being helped by medication, only to discover the side affects kept them from taking it.) Here is what I have learned: In every situation we can rely on God's love, grace and strength. If God has not given us relief from some challenge, there is still more he has to teach us in the midst of it. It may seem almost unbearable, but he will always be enough.

In my case, I am convinced that God allowed me to go through some very painful times to teach me some deep and lasting lessons, and then in "due time" he lifted me up. He may have you in his kiln right now. He may have had you there longer than you think is reasonable. But I can tell you he is not unfair and he has not forgotten you. If you stay humble under his mighty hand, in due time he will lift you also. And when he lifts you up, you will not just be relieved. You will be wiser and stronger.

> And the God of all grace, who called you to his eternal glory in Christ, after you have suffered a little while, will himself restore you and make you strong, firm and steadfast. To him be the power for ever and ever. Amen.
>
> *1 Peter 5:10-11*

6

In Due Time

Humble yourself, therefore, under God's mighty hand, that
he may lift you up in due time.

1 Peter 5:6

Once life has dealt us a difficult hand of cards, we can
become impatient, wondering when the deck will be reshuffled
and when we will get a new deal. What I have come to understand is that I do not compose the timetable for my life or for
the lives of those whom I love. The Bible tells us, to God "a day
is like a thousand years, and a thousand years are like a day" (2
Peter 3:8).

First and Second Peter are full of admonitions to persevere
under suffering. How can our childish minds comprehend this?
Especially when the suffering is so severe? God has to continuously guide us to keep his perspective on suffering. From
his eternal perspective, I'm sure that we seem like little children who have very little sense of time and keep asking, "Are
we there yet?"

Because of what we have been through as a family, my
perspective on the duration of suffering has changed. Things
that used to really bother me and be a big deal just aren't
anymore. Burned toast used to set my day on a downward spiral, but after watching my son go through three years of chemotherapy, I've learned to *get a grip.* I take things more in
stride. At times, I can even find myself a little impatient when
mothers complain about staying up all night with a sick child.
Because God has allowed me to suffer, I can usually maintain
a godly perspective and help others get a grip as well.

But when it comes to seeing someone I love, especially my
child, deal with chronic pain, my "grip" is harder to get.

No End in Sight

Michael and I are fortunate in that our cancers had an end-
ing point. After a five-year period with no relapse, cancer is

considered cured. We had a specific illness with a specific diagnosis and a specific treatment that would either cure us or
not, certainly within the framework of the will of God. In other
words, you get better or you die.

Our daughter, Christie, however, had a different type of
challenge ahead of her, one that was not easily diagnosed or
treated. Our perky, talented, athletic and spiritual teenager
began complaining of headaches, stomach aches, fatigue and
just generally not feeling well every morning. It was frustrating to us because she would always feel great later in the day.
We thought maybe she was just avoiding school. For weeks, in
spite of her protests of feeling lousy, we made her go to school
day after day. Actually, life was feeling pretty lousy for all of
us at that point.

I knew that she was not handling my illness and her own
problems very well. She seemed to be out of touch with reality. I remember shaking her one day and saying, "Christie, do
you realize that I have cancer. I might die. Does it matter to
you?" That was probably not the best approach to help her get
back in touch, but I simply did not know how to reach her.

In our minds, Christie had overreacted to traumas in the
past. In retrospect, we realize that at that point she was probably the only one being real with her emotions. At ten, when
Michael was diagnosed with leukemia, she was old enough to
understand that people die from it. Her fears of death blos-
somed in the middle of the night. Many, many nights she would
come crying to our room and wake me up saying she didn't
feel good. Her allergies did cause her sore throats and other
problems, but to me her problems were very *fixable.*

Finally, I realized there was more going on. When I got
coherent enough to talk her through what was really bother-
ing her, she confided, "David got sick with the croup last year
and was in the hospital for five days. Next, Michael got leukemia, and that's worse than croup. Now it's my turn to get something bad, and it will be worse than Michael's sickness, and I
will probably die."

From that point on I could see why she would panic whenever she got sick. If Michael ran a fever, we had to rush him to the emergency room, but if Christie got a fever we would give her a few baby aspirins and tell her to rest. In her mind, we were totally missing the seriousness of her condition and were standing idly by as she could be dying. Now at sixteen years old, she felt we were missing the seriousness of her condition again. This time she was right!

Our Eyes Were Opened

During this time she felt extremely alone and frightened. Her dad and I were trying to deal with my cancer. I could barely stay focused on the basics of life at that point. I realize now the incredible impact that a life challenge for one family member has on every single member of the family. The emotional needs of children and spouses need to be addressed as well as the patient's needs. Suffering is not isolated. We were not as "in tune" to her needs emotionally or physically as we needed to be.

One of the reasons we were not in tune with her was that none of us were being very "real" at this point. (In Chapter 11 we will discuss the necessity of being truthful and real to promote healing.) Her frequent asthma attacks and allergies received treatment because they were obvious problems. But that was all that we knew how to treat. She did not feel heard or believed when she tried to tell us that she was sick.

Praise God! Chelly Larson, Christie's teen ministry leader, got involved and listened to her! She opened up to Chelly about all her fears and guilt. Chelly, in turn, helped to open our eyes and ears to see Christie's pain.

At this point, Christie was suffering every day with severe headaches, frequent infections, debilitating pain, as well as extreme fatigue. We finally discovered that she was suffering from fibromyalgia[1] and endometriosis.[2] In essence, her immune system was shot. She was finally diagnosed with Chronic Fatigue Immune Dysfunction Syndrome (CFIDS).

Our doctor told us that younger women with endometriosis experience more painful symptoms than older women. To date, Christie has had three surgeries and numerous hormone treatments to try to get it under control. The hormone treatments were a serious assault on her emotional and physical state. My surgery had thrown me into sudden menopause, and her medication had caused temporary, menopausal-type symptoms. Needless to say, this was definitely *not* a "bonding experience." She also had ovarian cysts that burst causing us to think that she was experiencing appendicitis attacks or worse.

Some of the treatments that she underwent seemed worse than the diseases. One doctor gave her medication that caused her to gain fifty pounds, compounding the discouragement that she already felt. When Roger and I could tell that these treatments were altering her very state of mind, we insisted that she get off everything but the essentials and go after a more holistic approach to build up her immune system.

I was hesitant to mention CFIDS by name because it elicits such an array of emotion-laden reactions such as, "Well, I get tired too," "She should just get more sleep," and "It is not a definitive diagnosis because there is no blood test for it."

Like Lupus and Epstein-Barr, CFIDS is a condition that results from a defective and weakened immune system. The diagnosis is determined as a result of testing and eliminating other possibilities. The treatment of immune deficiencies is an insidious proposition. It is like the phenomenon that fire fighters call "ground fire" or "hot spots": just as they get one area of a forest fire under control, it pops up in another area. To give us a perspective on how Christie was feeling, her doctor described CFIDS this way; "Do you know how you feel on the first day of the flu? You get aches, pains, headaches and fatigue. Well, that is how Christie's body feels. It is like fighting the flu every day of her life. Her body is in a constant attack mode."

One of the most deceiving aspects of CFIDS is that the patient displays no external symptoms. There is no rash or obvious evidence other than extreme fatigue. The other barb is that when the person feels good, he or she feels really good, and onlookers may think that there is really nothing wrong.

Are We There Yet?

Christie's devastating conditions have continued through the last seven years. Her physical challenges have kept her from completing the educational and career goals she had set. Yet, watching her deal with these illnesses has brought about a deeper understanding of chronic suffering. Enduring temporary pain and temporary fatigue at least has an end, but many people suffer without that luxury of anticipating future peace, without anticipating an earthly end to their suffering. Apparently, the apostle Paul had a "thorn in the flesh" that would not go away. In 2 Corinthians 12:7-10, God told him, "My grace is sufficient for you, for my power is made perfect in weakness." That is a noble thought that can frequently be dulled by daily pain and fatigue. Feelings of uselessness to God, ourselves and others can consume the thoughts of those of us who are physically challenged, especially if we have little hope of *not* being physically challenged.

No matter what is happening to us or to our bodies, we must hold on to our faith that God's grace is sufficient for us. We must believe that his strength is sufficient for each moment of pain—not that this is easy. Waking up every day with intense pain is hard. Waking up feeling physically and emotionally defeated before the day begins can be overwhelming. But, that is the moment that our commitment to love God with all our heart, soul, mind and strength is tested.

Christie has shared that her illnesses caused her to be even more determined to love and trust God. "I had to trust God," she said. "He was the only one who really knew what I was going through. He was my only source of hope so many times. I cannot imagine how hard life would be without him."

On Her Own

A time came when I had to realize that Christie had faith enough and was strong enough to fight her own battles. It was time for me to "let go" and surrender her to God's care. I had done all that I could do. I had bought enough vitamins and "good health" books to put one of us through medical school. In my eagerness to battle her illness, I tried to take over too much. She had to take on the responsibility for her own health and spiritual well-being. I think she was ready to do that before I was ready to let her.

My desire to fix the wounded actually goes back to my childhood days when the boys in the neighborhood always made me be the nurse when we played "war." When someone was "wounded," I would run out on the battlefield, hover over them and say, "Fix! Fix!" Then they would jump up, all better again, and run back into the battle. I guess I wanted to be able to say, "Fix! Fix!" over Christie. It just didn't seem to work that way in real life.

During her early twenties Christie cut the apron strings. She was having excruciating tooth pain which sent me into my "Mother Protector" role. I called a dentist whom she had not seen for years because her current dentist was not responding quickly enough to suit me. When I spoke to her old dentist, he had too many questions for me to answer, so I handed Christie the phone. Then I heard Christie say in a very grown-up voice, "I am sorry that my mother bothered you with this. I have already contacted my dentist, and I am sure he will be calling soon."

Lights flashed! Bells rang! Oh, no! I had become one of *those* mothers. Frankly, her health has improved since she has taken charge of it herself.

Bad Times and Good Times

Following through every day on our commitment to love God, in sickness and in health, keeps us going in spite of our feelings. The blessing that comes from our obedience, in spite of our circumstances (for better or for worse), often allows us to "feel better."

I learned this lesson in our twenty-seven-year marriage relationship many years ago: "It is commitment that keeps love in a marriage rather than love that keeps us committed." Our feelings can change moment by moment, but our commitment will keep us steady "till death do us part." This is a lesson that Christie is also learning.

She also knows the value of staying committed during the good times: "Sometimes, when I am feeling good, I am tempted to become self-reliant again. Going through these illnesses has taught me to see how God must work in our daily lives. I can be very self-confident instead of God-confident.

God knew that I have always desired to work in some capacity in the full-time ministry. He also knew what he was dealing with in my sinful nature. In my determination, I could easily go running off on a spiritual quest and forget to include God. John 15 tells us that we will never bear fruit unless we stay connected to God. It is very sobering for me to see how my illnesses are a necessary *blessing."*

Outward Focus

When Christie was able to accept her long-term prognosis, she began to work creatively within it. I was amazed by her focus on others in the midst of her pain. She discovered that keeping an outward focus kept her mind off herself and her pain. Her attitude was, "I can be with other people and be in pain, or I can be at home alone and still be in pain." When she was tired or in pain to the point of it being a distraction to others, she would rest alone. I saw her rely on God to get her through situations when she needed to "seek first the kingdom." It was obvious that God was giving her the strength to do it.

Christie and I both have learned from godly women, such as Pat Gempel and Elena McKean, to rely on God through incredibly difficult situations. We have seen these women push through pain, sleepless nights, family illness as well as the neglect of personal comfort to see that the needs of the kingdom of God are met.

Just Give Your Best

Christie had to work through many feelings about her worth and value as a person as well as a disciple. As she worked through personal feelings of uselessness, she became concerned

about what others would think of her. She knew she was doing all that she could do, but would others understand?

Ultimately, what she had to realize was that it comes down
to just her and what God knows about her. When Jesus saw the
widow give her pitiful few pennies in the offering, he was impressed that she had given all that she had to give. When all
that you have is a few good hours a day, and you give that to
God, won't that be pleasing to God and to the people who
really are trying to please God too? Many disciples helped her
to learn this lesson. People like Roy and Chelly Larson, Andy
and Stacie Yeatman, and Kevin and Debbie McDaniel all believed in her and helped her to grow.

God has blessed Christie's perseverance and faith. During
a recent exploratory surgery it was discovered that her endometriosis was completely gone and that the doctor's con-
cerns about possible intestinal disease were unfounded. She
still battles a weakened immune system, but even that is im-
proving. In spite of her physical limits, God has expanded the
borders of her faith. She is now working in the full-time campus ministry. In due time God has helped her weather her life
storm and has made her spiritually strong, firm and steadfast
(1 Peter 5:10).

A Spiritual Perspective

Which is better? It is better, by far, to be spiritually strong
and physically weak than to be spiritually weak and physically
strong. The greatest moment in Jesus' life was when he could
physically do nothing. He was nailed to a cross. But from his
cross he inspired us to love God with our whole heart; he forgave us; he held on to his faith in God; he expressed his love;
he obeyed; he trusted God with his future; he did not sin; he
took up our sorrows and infirmities; he suffered for our sake,
and he opened the door to heaven for us. He did not whine, "Is
it almost over?" He knew it would be over when God's will
was finally done in his life. At that point, he submitted his last
breath and said, "Father, into your hands I commit my spirit."

In Due Time

We are quick to hold God to his promises. We want them met "now," but when we are the ones making the promises, we hold ourselves to a much more lenient standard, such as when we have nothing else "due" or nothing else "to do." (And when does that ever happen?)

God uses the term "in due time" to remind us to be patient in waiting for his answers because he has reasons for making us wait. Peter reminds us, "Humble yourself, therefore, under God's mighty hand, that he may lift you up *in due time*...And the God of all grace who called you to his eternal glory in Christ, after you have suffered *a little while*, will himself restore you and make you strong, firm and steadfast" (1 Peter 5:6, 10, emphasis added).

His "due time" and mine are often not the same, especially when it comes to my suffering or the suffering of those whom I love. His "little while" and mine are often not the same length of time, especially when I or those I love are hurting. But only God knows when lessons have been learned, when faith and trust have sufficiently been refined and when perseverance has been practiced enough to deeply integrate his love and wisdom into our lives. In God's perspective of eternity, he knows the right time to restore us, and just about the time that occurs, it's "due time" for another lesson. But, thankfully, he never sends us a new one until we are strong enough to handle it.

7

Hoop Dreams: Time Out

All your sons will be taught by the LORD,
and great will be your children's peace.

Isaiah 54:13

"Be strong in your heart or be weak in commitment. Commitment must be based on moral integrity and sound character. Your reputation is what people think you are; your character is what God knows you to be. Your choices reflect your character."

The preceding is a quote handwritten in the back of my Bible. I don't know who first wrote it or said it, but God wanted me to engrave it in my heart.

When God started working on my character, I felt as though I had as much strength as melted Jell-O. People-pleasing, anxiety, fear, worry, double-mindedness, inconsistency and lack of discipline were some of my traits (of course, I was also very proud of my humble self-righteousness).

Time for Testing

As God worked on my character, he tested my love for him. Tests are not so much to prove to God how much we love him—I think he already knows that. Rather, they come to show *us* how much we love God. And when they come, our progress *and* our weak points also show up.

One of my tests was much like the one sent to Abraham thousands of years ago. The setting was not on the top of a mountain beside a hastily built altar, though. It was at an evangelism seminar in Florida. The night of the big formal banquet came, and I was looking forward to attending the dress-up occasion with my husband. Childcare was graciously provided on site. When I arrived at the hotel room we were using as a nursery to drop off our baby, Michael, I realized it was grossly understaffed. My heart would not let me leave all those babies with just a few young women. So, there I was in my formal gown, changing diapers and giving bottles.

But before long, the tranquillity of the room was destroyed by a blaring fire alarm. I went out into the hallway and felt a sickening blast of hot air. *The babies! How will we get all the babies out?* I thought. Each of the other adults quickly grabbed three babies and headed for the stairs.

There were four babies left after all the others had been taken. Just four babies and me! I tried in vain to hold four of them. Then came the moment of true faith. *Which baby will I leave?* With tears and anguish I said good-bye to *my* baby. I knew that he would be with God if the worst happened. I didn't know how strong the other mothers' faith was. How could I explain leaving someone else's child behind and taking mine? In tears, I rushed out the door and started down the ten flights of stairs.

By God's sovereign power and will, the singers for the evening's program were on the ninth floor and were exiting by the same stairwell. Recognizing one of the women, I asked if she and the other singers would each take a baby down to safety. They each unburdened the full arms of the baby-sitters, including mine.

Then I rushed back up to Michael with gratitude to God. That moment struck a chord deep in my heart that would lay the foundation for my trust and surrender of my children's welfare into God's mighty hands. I knew from that day on that God loves my children even more than I do.

When Michael developed leukemia at age six, my whole-hearted love for God was tested again (see Chapter 1). During that ordeal, we had prayed that if Michael were going to grow up and deny God at some point, then we would be willing for God to take him now as a innocent child, although it would hurt terribly. Praise God he made it to his cure date and beyond. Life was looking great!

Again, Lord?

Through the years, participating in sports has been a great joy for Michael. His natural athletic talents, along with the determined spirit he developed from fighting leukemia, gave him a winner's edge in many sports. He played soccer, basketball, football and lacrosse and was named "Unsung Hero of the Year" for all sports in junior high. He received many other honors, including "Best Defensive Player" in lacrosse and football, but basketball was his first love.

During Michael's junior year of high school, he went through varsity basketball tryouts with the usual butterflies. During this process, the coach reminded me that we had failed to get the required physical examination to show that Michael was able to participate in competitive sports. The coach was very concerned because he loved Michael's team attitude and all-out aggressive style of play, and would probably use him as a starter. Since we needed the medical permission quickly, I called his doctor at the Dana Farber Cancer Institute in Boston. Michael had recently had his annual checkup there, and I thought he could surely fax a letter of permission. But this conscientious oncologist wanted Michael to go through another cardiology study at the Boston Children's Hospital before he would give his approval.

"Remember, Mrs. Lamb," he said, "we are watching his heart for evidence of damage and stress due to the chemotherapy he had as a child."

The day after the heart tests, the cardiologist called and asked me to put Michael on the phone too. The results showed significant deterioration of his heart function. Later, in the doctor's office, we learned that Michael was in the beginning stages of congestive heart failure, meaning that his heart was congested with fluid and was, therefore, under extreme pressure. If not treated with medication and curtailed activity, this condition can result in death. His doctor consulted with other cardiologists, and they all agreed soundly: no competitive sports. His cancer cure had come at a great personal cost to a junior in high school.

Looking at the facts, and consulting with the doctors until we were convinced that they were right, we all felt grateful that God had stopped a probable tragedy. But emotionally it was hard to watch Michael struggle through the pain of giving up sports—the source of so much of his confidence and sense of victory over cancer. Now it was sports that could take his life.

Spiritual Battle

At a deeper level of Michael's heart, another battle was raging—a spiritual one. I prayed more over this contest than the physical contests for his health. Just like a mom at her child's ball games, I had to watch patiently, and cheer him from the sidelines in his spiritual struggles. Ultimately, though, I simply had to trust God. Just as in the hotel room years earlier, I had to surrender Michael to God. When Michael had chosen to become a disciple and be baptized on August 2, 1989, he chose God to be his head coach and referee, not me. As much as I wanted to, I could not compete in Michael's place.

After he had been a disciple a short time, he began to feel the pull of the world. The pressure of being a popular athlete was pushing out the wholehearted commitment to being a disciple that he once had. Wanting to be liked by everyone divided his heart. He saw being a teen Christian as a hindrance to his potential success as an athlete and to his popularity with his classmates. No amount of talking would convince him otherwise.

Michael developed an "attitude" toward God. From his perspective, every time he personally made progress in his confidence and abilities, God knocked him down. Michael is one of those students who has to work extremely hard in school. He can approach tests feeling great about what he knows and then get very disappointing results. So, in academics he felt "knocked down."

Because of ministry needs, our family moved frequently, bringing with each move the challenge of building new friendships and a new reputation. He felt that he started at a knocked-down disadvantage every time we moved.

But sports gave Michael an edge on making friends and gaining respect quickly. When sports were taken away from him, he felt that God was taking too much this time. He even rationalized that through sports he would be able to give God attention and glory. But that was Michael's plan for this stage in his life, not God's plan.

Not understanding and trusting God's purpose, Michael fought God and carried a personal grudge against him. He felt hurt, angry and disappointed. He felt he had suffered enough. If this was God's idea of a spiritual cure, the cost was too much to bear. It simply did not feel like love.

I clung to my faith in the God who had spared Michael as an infant and again spared him as a child. When we had prayed that God would take him as a child if he would not later be a faithful disciple, we had no idea that this spiritual battle would be in his future or ours. Every teen must come to his own personal faith and commitment to God, but I felt myself fighting panic as I saw him handle his spiritual life with less care than his physical life.

In his preliminary writing for the teen devotional book, *Let It Shine*,[1] Michael reflected on a moment that was a significant turning point for him in coping with the cost of his cure:

> During this time I was very humbled and realized how fragile life really is. I will never forget coming back from playing a full-court basketball game at a YMCA in Tennessee when I heard that Reggie Lewis, the twenty-seven-year-old Celtics captain, had collapsed and died of heart failure on the spot. It really scared me. I had so many questions, 'Why wasn't it me who was taken?'"

The reality of Reggie's death made Michael realize the unique camaraderie he had with God's Son. Jesus offered us the cure for our spiritual cancer, and he paid the high price for that cure. Michael was beginning to get an eternal perspective on this game of life again; he renewed his love and commitment to God.

Most Valuable Player

In spite of his heart condition, Michael was asked to stay on the high school basketball team as an "injured player" for the next two seasons. His varsity coach commended him in a feature article in the Boston Globe as their "most valuable player" because of his spirit and commitment to the team, even though he was never able to play a game. We had once hoped that Michael's athletic abilities would enable him to earn a college scholarship, but God had a better plan. At graduation he was awarded two scholarships; one was for "character" and the other was for his leadership in the D.A.R.E. program (Drug Abuse Resistance Education) with elementary school children.

When it came time for Michael to choose a college, he looked at the many great campus ministries first. He wanted to be sure that he would be challenged to grow spiritually. He is now attending UCLA where he is an effective student leader in the campus ministry. He is a part of a soul-winning team with the promise of an eternal victory.

God loves to give "rewards" too (Hebrews 11:6). Michael's doctors have been so impressed with his physical improvement that they have okayed his return to sports. He is now a strong and vital part of the UCLA lacrosse team.

God has taught me to trust him as he has worked to develop my character. Several times during this game of life, God has had to call "time out" to show me that his game plan also included training the personal integrity and character of my children. Those have been the moments in life when I have been the most tempted to take over and try to coach God. Thankfully, however, God's sovereign power and wisdom and coaching always produces great victories. Throughout all our family has suffered, we have come to confidently know one thing: Hope in God will never disappoint us.

8

The Eye of the Storm
From Roger's Perspective

Each man will be like a shelter from the wind
    and a refuge from the storm,
like streams of water in the desert
    and the shadow of a great rock in a thirsty land.
Isaiah 32:2

Because David, our youngest, was in preschool, he would often accompany Marcia and me on the 300-mile round-trip to St. Louis Children's Hospital for Michael's treatments. These dreaded events occurred two to three times per week the first summer, tapering off to once per week and then once per month over subsequent years. David's presence was a delight because of his constantly joyful and empathetic spirit.

Michael and David were so close that Michael wanted him in the room with him during the cataclysmic event. David would crawl under the treatment table and busy himself with Superman (or the hero of the day) while Michael dealt with the torture of the day—chemo injections, bone marrows, spinal taps or any combination of these.

On one memorable occasion, David taught all of us about being a great friend to those who suffer. The nurse was preparing to give Michael two shots to prepare him for a bone marrow procedure. You cannot anesthetize the bone from which the marrow is being extracted, but you can numb the skin, which is important since the instrument used is a small stainless steel pipe that is shoved into the bone at the back of the pelvis. The nurse told Michael, "When I count to three, say 'Ouch.'" As she counted to three and gave him the injection, Michael proved that he had already learned the meaning of "macho"—he simply clenched his teeth and scowled in the best Clint Eastwood imitation ever. "Now, you didn't say, 'Ouch.' I'll count to three again. One, two, three..." And from underneath the table came the bravest little "Ouch" you ever heard.

In so many ways this simple anecdote illustrates the crucial role close relationships play to those who are suffering. Loved ones in pain don't need pity, investigation or condemnation. They need us to be *with* them and to *lay down our lives* for them. They need us to be the eye in the center of the storm blowing their emotions and bodies around. Some of the saddest stories ever told are about people in the middle of turmoil who try to lean on their relationships for support only to find them crumbling or absent.

Being There

When the doctors left the room after telling Marcia and me that Michael had leukemia, my mind and my heart were swirling with outrageous thoughts. Shane, the next-door neighbors' boy, Michael's best friend, had just died of leukemia. *We probably won't see Mike's seventh birthday. What do we say to him? To our other children? How do I comfort Marcia? How do I tell my parents? Her parents? Shane's parents? How do we tell the church? How do we pay for this? How do we encourage the doctors who seemed so devastated by the diagnosis? Who do we turn to for help?*

Marcia and I held each other, then dropped to our knees to pray. As we were crying and praying, it was so good to be talking with God as a loving Father instead of just someone we were grasping for in desperation.

Then it was time for the difficult phone calls. I picked up the receiver in the doctors' lounge where we were huddled and waited for the instructions on how to get an outside line. While on hold, I noticed several textbooks on leukemia. As I numbly thumbed through them, the name of Dr. Theresa Vietti appeared repeatedly as an author, editor, writer and source. It was as though God had put his arm around us and said, "I am with you." The doctors rotated taking new patients on different days and that Tuesday Dr. Vietti was seeing new leukemia patients. She turned out to be not only an incredible person, but also the head of the Pediatric Oncology Department at St. Louis Children's Hospital. We would later find out that she had been in the leukemia field more than twenty years and was chairman of a vital research group which helped to link research hospitals throughout the entire country. We also found out that a Christian in the church in Florida was her right-hand statistician. During the course of treatment, he prayed as he kept constant watch over Mike's progress. Feeling and knowing that God was present gave us the example and the strength to be what Michael needed from the beginning. Whenever I was at a loss as to how to comfort him, I simply thought, *How has God comforted me?* (2 Corinthians 1:3-7).

Both of our families were incredibly supportive—totally encouraging us and ready to sacrifice anything. Both Marcia's parents and my parents have been married for fifty-two years. The stability their influence has given us is irreplaceable. And they, as couples, are best friends with each other.

My parents have always been there for me. But they have also been there for others. When I was growing up, we regularly had people into our home for a meal a few times a week. We were often in other people's homes, too. My parents could always be counted on to host a teen party or a church function. Both of them are excellent cooks, and because of their willingness to take care of others, multitudes of sick and lonely people benefited. One thing that stuck with me all these years was going with my mom to visit sick people—and those we used to call "shut-ins." She would be observant of every little need they had. Most of all she would listen to them, care for them and love them. I didn't realize it then, but I was learning how to "be there" for people. I also have an incredible sister, Gail, who has Down's Syndrome. From the time I can first remember, I have seen my parents love her and put her needs above their own, placing her in the best situations for her to achieve her full potential. She is one of the real joys of our family and quickly becomes the beloved queen of any school or living arrangement she is in. From my parents and Gail, I have learned innumerable practical lessons in compassion.

After talking with our parents about Michael's illness, I called my best friend, Kip McKean. Our relationship had begun a few years earlier when I hired him to be the campus minister at our little church in Charleston, Illinois. He came into town with a fire in his eye and a passion in his heart that I envied. He also came needing my support as the pulpit minister because of the way he had been mistreated by the previous church he served. Needless to say, we had our bumps. I finally came to a point where I decided that one of three things needed to happen: he would leave, I would leave or I would have to make some changes in my life. I had never seen anyone as sold out for God and as effective in helping others with their own relationships with God. People were making radical decisions and changes, and I had to either be one of them or walk away from God. I finally faced my religious pride and admitted where I really was spiritually. Along with the church, we went through a lot together. We learned from the Scriptures how to love each other deeply and be truly united with each other.

As I was dialing to talk with Kip and Elena, I was so grateful that God had brought him into my life to challenge the integrity of my faith. Here we were facing the worst thing ever to happen to us spiritually, and we had the faith, commitment and love to see it through. That wouldn't have been true just a short time before. I knew they would want to know about Michael and we needed their prayers and support. The irony of the phone call cemented our relationship forever. I don't remember who shared their news first, but I will never forget experiencing such incredible joy and incredible pain at the same moment. Elena had just given birth to their first child, Olivia, on Michael's birthday the day before. They had been trying to reach us to share their good news. We celebrated her birth and mourned Michael's possible death. It truly was rejoicing with those who rejoice and weeping with those who weep. This was the love that I had heard about and even taught about, but previously had never really experienced myself. This is why Olivia's birthdays have such a special meaning to us. We were there at her spiritual birth in the Pacific Ocean in 1995, and although everyone was rejoicing, I think our smiles were a bit different from the rest of the crowd's. God has been and is still here with us because Kip and Elena called us to be there for God.

"Being there" for someone means different things to different people. Marcia and I discovered this the first week of Mike's diagnosis. We were sleeping on the floor of his room in St. Louis, waking every morning with the realization this was not just a bad dream. Our bodies ached from the floor, but our hearts ached more as Mike went through series after series of tests and treatments. We watched helplessly as our son grew sicker—this time from the medicine. I have never seen a mother do a better job of being there for her children in a serious illness. Marcia has honestly shared some of her struggles with you in this book, but in the hour of crisis she was tuned in to what Michael was thinking and feeling—a definite gift she has with children. On the other hand, I was focusing on soothing any of Mike's and Marcia's fears, trying to take care of all the physical arrangements so they wouldn't have to think about them. I was trying to show strength, hope and faith in the dark. It was my way of being there for them. Later, Marcia asked me, "Why don't you cry?"

Suddenly it hit me. I was so busy being strong *for* them that I had failed to let them see I was hurting *with* them. "Marcia, I have been crying in the shower every day," I confided. I learned that being there for someone means to hurt with them first, then to take care of them.

Lay Down Your Life

I believe there are certain defining moments in everyone's life. They reveal the most about who we really are and what we really believe deep in our gut. These defining moments come in different forms. For our family they have come mostly in the form of illnesses and Pharisees. We'll save the Pharisees for another book. But when Michael's illness struck, it revealed that our faith in God was genuine. I am still sobered by memories of the numerous families we saw crumble when their lives were tested. I can still see the hurt in the eyes of one mother whose husband left her one week after losing their daughter to leukemia. But for the grace of God sending Kip and Elena into our lives, that is where we could have been. When Michael was pronounced cured five years later, we were coleading a new church in Chicago with Marty and Chris Fuqua, who had become disciples in Charleston. The church exploded from 300 to 1500 in three years. God answered the prayers of his people all over the world for Michael, and we had started a church in Champaign, Illinois—the sky was the limit in Chicago! God's movement was starting to multiply after years of tough, slow growth. Entire churches were asking to be taught about being true disciples.

The next defining moment was like being broadsided by a truck. "Your wife has cancer." Every painful experience of Michael's leukemia flooded my mind. *Wait a minute! I've been down this road. I've run this gauntlet. I've paid my dues. Not this. Not us. Not now.* I knew where these thoughts were coming from. The dark side is more real than Darth Vader. There is an actual spiritual battle, and we were in the middle of it. Satan had sent another messenger, and that one was soon followed by another: Only one month after the surgery, one of the men we had sent to lead a mission planting rebelled and tried to divide our churches. The Fuquas had to quickly move to St. Louis to lead that church for a few months. Meanwhile, I needed to lead the Chicago church, put together a retreat for the Midwest church leaders and lead the first of several "reconstructions" in which entire churches were becoming discipling ministries. The devil was trying to take us out by getting us to doubt God. He made a flank attack just when we thought we were in the clear. He was trying to destroy not only our faith, but the faith of all the people who had prayed for us and believed in God's faithfulness. As Moses pled with God in the wilderness, we pled with God not to allow his name to be dishonored. I was determined that I would not let this attack deter me from his purpose. We would defeat the enemy again by relying on God. What I didn't realize was the depth of the lesson that God was preparing for me.

Throughout Michael's leukemia, I learned a lot of basics

about being there for people when they are suffering. With Marcia's cancer, I felt like I was sent to graduate school in learning about who I really was and what my convictions were. Our entire life changed. Marcia went through a radical hysterectomy and seven weeks of radiation burning inside her entire abdomen in case there were any hidden cancer cells. She had no estrogen, constant body pain and a severe loss of body fluids. She barely had any strength. As she put it, she felt like she had PMS *every* day—for three years.

After a few months, it became apparent that this was not going to be a short-term problem—we would have to radically change our life-styles. Although things were challenging, I still felt that slowing down on my ministry responsibilities would be giving in to the enemy. Then we had a fateful talk with Marty and Chris Fuqua and John and Nancy Mannel. (We had studied the Bible with the Mannels and baptized them in Charleston. Now he served with me as an elder in the Chicago church.) They asked me what I would be willing to give up for Marcia. In truth, I hadn't thought of it that way. I had thought of not giving in to the enemy. I was confused and defensive until Marcia shared something that cut to the very core of my heart. Marty asked Marcia how she felt and she said, "Do you remember that scene in the movie, *Vacation,* where the dog is accidentally tied to the bumper and they all get in the car and take off down the highway? Well, that's how I feel."

I practically slid underneath the chair and looked up at her like a dog that had just discovered he had made a mess on the carpet. I felt terrible. I had been so focused on laying my life down in the battle for men's souls that I had forgotten to lay down my life for the one soul I vowed to God to protect more than any other.

I'll Be There for You

The church was the true family of God in serving and providing for our physical, emotional and spiritual needs. As life returned to some semblance of a routine around the house, we divided up some of Marcia's responsibilities to take pressure off her. Each family member learned to do his or her own laundry at a very young age. We took on more of the cleaning and cooking. Those were natural ways to serve that actually benefited each one of us. Later, when Christie and Michael left home, they had a head start on their roommates in running a household.

Ten months after Marcia's surgery, we celebrated our twentieth wedding anniversary by restating our vows in a touching ceremony in our backyard. Our children, our closest friends and my parents were there. Having your own kids hear you vow to love each other "for better or worse, for richer or poorer, in sickness and in health" is an incomparable joy. But living it out before them is even better. The test had come in staying true to my commitment when, after the surgery, Marcia was not the vibrant, funny, warm person I had fallen in love with. On our wedding day as I watched her walk toward me on a sunlit afternoon, I remembered the day I had met her at four in the afternoon where the three sidewalks crossed in front of the student union the first week of college. (She doesn't remember it at all.) Her incredible warmth and great smile won my heart from that moment. We married before our senior year of college.

Just when our family had overcome a great challenge, just when the kids were going into their teen years, just when we were being used by God more than ever, just when his movement was really picking up speed—everything suddenly changed. Marcia had suffered from depression and anxiety before becoming a true disciple. Afterward she really started to shine. But after the surgery, estrogen deprivation caused a loss in her zest for life, along with other problems such as a diminished sex drive and dry irritable skin. Her despair reappeared. She wondered if it would be better for her to die. She even wondered if God was done with her now. Due to the estrogen problem and the effects of radiation, she was in extreme pain every time we were intimate. Often her skin would be hurt by just an affectionate touch.

The reality of our vows to God came home. *What if this is our life from now on? What if things don't ever get any better?*

What if her vibrancy never returns and we will never be able to have sex again without pain? I looked at the definition of marriage in Ephesians 5:25, "Husbands love your wives just as Christ loved the church, and gave himself up for her...." Wedding vows always end with "until death do us part." We had taught these truths in numerous classes and counseling sessions. These truths had totally transformed our marriage years earlier when we first decided to totally commit our lives to God. I never envisioned how I would really need to live them out. I had vowed to love God first for the rest of my life. I had vowed to be a true disciple of Jesus by his definition: "If anyone would come after me, he must deny himself and take up his cross daily and follow me" (Luke 9:23). Was I really willing to lay my life down for my wife?

I was bombarded with thoughts of how it might have been different, of whether it was fair or not, of self-pity for having my plans changed and about a million more alternatives. Now my word was on the line. I had vowed to God to be a disciple and a husband—for better or for worse. This was definitely worse. But that didn't change my vow.

In 1995 I was able to spend nearly a week in Jerusalem during Passover and Easter. Walking through the Garden of Gethsemane is a profoundly humbling experience. I was reminded of my own earlier struggle with keeping my vow. During those times, in my heart I had been with Jesus in the Garden. I realized that he was faced with not just the physical agony of the cross, but also with taking on the sins of the world, which would separate him from God for a time. He was about to be humiliated and tortured simply for being righteous. He would be ridiculed by the very people he was dying to save. Suddenly my cross seemed much lighter than I had thought. Jesus had struggled with bearing the sins of those who hated him, and I had struggled with giving my heart to the one person in the whole world who had vowed to love me as the church loved Christ, who had entrusted her life to me, borne me three incredible children, given her life to follow Jesus, nurtured Michael through his illness, loved me when I was unlovable and believed in me more than anyone else in the whole world. Now she was hurting and she needed me, my love, my devotion.

I realized what I had struggled with. I had been afraid. Afraid my life wouldn't turn out as I wanted it to. Afraid of all the pain of Michael's illness being dredged up again, but not having a partner to bear it with. Afraid that I could not nurture her the way she had nurtured Michael. Afraid of laying my life down in ways I had never dreamed.

The Bible teaches there are two things that overcome fear—faith and love. With Michael I learned more about deep faith. With Marcia I learned more about true love. When that became clear, it seemed like the right things to do and say came naturally. When Marcia was despairing, somehow I knew what to say to reassure her of God's love and my love. When our sex life was so painful, I was afraid of hurting her physically, and she was afraid of hurting me emotionally. I told her that it didn't matter as long as we could be together.

A crucial decision came in 1990 when Marcia was not able to keep up with the pace of the ministry. My lifetime dreams and goals in the ministry came face to face with reality. We prayed and gave it over to God. I had to let it go. I was preparing to go to law school or do some other mid-life crisis thing when God intervened. Kip McKean called and said he wanted me to be the editor of *Discipleship Magazine*, which we later developed into *UpsideDown Magazine*. Marcia was blessed with two years of healing and the personal stimulation of teaching children again in the top inclusion preschool in New England (including special education students in regular classrooms). Then God began Kingdom News Network, and we were asked to move to Los Angeles to direct it. Now I serve as Director of Media for the International Churches of Christ, producer and writer of the video news magazine, and as managing editor of *L.A. Story*, a publication for all the leaders of the churches in more than ninety countries. God has a great sense of humor. Our years in the ministry, my graduate work in communications, our inclination to write, our love for the big picture of the kingdom of God, incredible relationships over the years—all of these have come together in God's dream for us. And the best part of all, my assistant editor on *L.A. Story* and assistant writer on KNN is Marcia. We have dueling laptops in our home office, and we have never had more fun or felt like we were contributing more.

To Sum It Up

The Cliff's Notes version of our story boils down to a passage in 2 Corinthians 12:7-10. In a nutshell, here is what we found:

1) *God does not send evil, the Devil does.* Paul called it "a thorn in the flesh, a messenger of Satan." Too often people give God the rap for the work of the dark side.

2) *God only allows evil to happen to us for our own good.* He allowed the thorn to be sent to Paul for two reasons: to keep him from becoming conceited and to teach him to rely on God. Spoiled children have everything smoothed out for them. God doesn't raise spoiled children.

3) *God's power is made perfect in weakness.* Every great man or woman has overcome adversity. The question is not "Will bad things happen to me?" but rather, "How will I react when bad things do happen to me?"

4) *None of us is good.* The biggest fallacy in the question, "Why do bad things keep happening to good people?" is that there are no truly good people. Paul also had a handle on it when he said, "All have sinned and fallen short of the glory of God (Romans 3:23)." God is the standard of goodness. Why do bad things happen to God?

5) *God's grace makes us good.* It is really all we need. Everything else we just want. When bad things happen, relying on God, the complete Goodness, is the answer to every question. Especially that big one, "Why me?"

If you were looking for a different answer, I'm sorry, but I've searched high and low and can't find another one. As a family, we have been grateful to learn that laying down our lives takes us through crosses to resurrections.

> The eyes of the LORD are on the righteous
>   and his ears are attentive to their cry;
> the face of the LORD is against those who do evil,
>   to cut off the memory of them from the earth.
> The righteous cry out, and the LORD hears them;
>   he delivers them from all their troubles.
> The LORD is close to the brokenhearted
>   and saves those who are crushed in spirit.

Psalm 34:15-18

Part 2

"Bad Things" Meet the Beatitudes

9

You Are Blessed

"But blessed is the man who trusts in the LORD,
whose confidence is in him."

Jeremiah 17:7

Jesus went throughout Galilee, teaching in their synagogues, preaching the good news of the kingdom, and healing every disease and sickness among the people. News about him spread all over Syria, and people brought to him all who were ill with various diseases, those suffering severe pain, the demon-possessed, those having seizures, and the paralyzed, and he healed them. Large crowds from Galilee, the Decapolis, Jerusalem, Judea and the region across the Jordan followed him. Now when he saw the crowds, he went up on a mountainside and sat down. His disciples came to him, and he began to teach them, saying:

"Blessed are the poor in spirit,
 for theirs is the kingdom of heaven.
Blessed are those who mourn,
 for they will be comforted.
Blessed are the meek,
 for they will inherit the earth.
Blessed are those who hunger
 and thirst for righteousness,
 for they will be filled.
Blessed are the merciful,
 for they will be shown mercy.
Blessed are the pure in heart,
 for they will see God.
Blessed are the peacemakers,
 for they will be called sons of God.
Blessed are those who are persecuted
 because of righteousness,
 for theirs is the kingdom of heaven.

"Blessed are you when people insult you, persecute you and falsely say all kinds of evil against you because of me. Rejoice and be glad, because great is your reward in heaven, for in the same way they persecuted the prophets who were before you."

Matthew 4:23-5:12

30 A.D....

The crowd quieted as the Master Teacher approached. An old woman wondered, *Will today be the day I witness a blind person healed?* A little boy was hoping to see a withered hand or leg restored to normal. So much had been said in the city about the miraculous power of this man. Questions were burning in the hearts and minds of the masses: *Is he from God? Is he a sorcerer from the devil as some are saying? How could he be doing so much good for God's people if he weren't from God?*

Looking into his eyes, they had never before seen such compassion from a righteous man. They were more familiar with the scornful glances of the Pharisees, making them feel like rejected sinners. As they watched him scan the crowd, they wondered what he might be thinking. *Is he looking for a well-known person to heal in order to validate his ministry? Perhaps he is looking for a righteous person who deserves to be healed.* They had seen his love for little children. *Surely he will heal a child today.* But to their amazement, Jesus slowly and deliberately walked a winding path through the crowd up a nearby hillside. There he sat down—he just sat down!

His disciples were probably as confused at their master's behavior as the now restless crowd was. *Doesn't Jesus realize this is the biggest crowd to date that has gathered to witness his miracles?* There were thousands of sick and needy people waiting hopefully for his healing touch. Judas had already computed the freewill offering that might be grossed that day. *Why is he just sitting there?*

Jesus turned to his bewildered disciples and, in essence, said, "These people are the blessed ones."

Now he has really flipped out! they must have thought. *He is looking at an enormous crowd of poor, crippled, blind people festering with grief, sorrow and hopelessness; and he calls them "blessed"! He must be going through Messiah burnout. He can't possibly mean what he's saying. Let's get him out of the hot sun, quick!*

Jesus slowly rose to his feet and began speaking boldly to the crowd. "You are blessed..."[1]

Before Peter could even have had a chance to grab Jesus' robe to pull him back down, Jesus had caught the attention of the crowd with his emotion-laden statement.

Murmurs must have run through the crowd. *What could this mean? Will he heal us all? Maybe he is going to set up a clinic right here so we don't have to keep following him around everywhere.* As they listened, they discovered that the words themselves seemed to carry their own healing. One by one the crowd settled to hear the words that were beginning to penetrate the layers of bandages surrounding their wounded spirits and hearts.

—————⟫●⟪—————

Why did Jesus choose this audience and this time in his ministry to present his most powerful sermon? Wouldn't the religious leaders of the day have appreciated it more? As Jesus later says most profoundly, "It is not the healthy who need a doctor, but the sick" (Matthew 9:12). The physically sick know they're sick. The funny thing is, the same is not always true of the spiritually sick. The Pharisees were told over and over again that they were the spiritually blind, but their spiritually deaf ears would not let them hear.

The beginning portion of the "Sermon on the Mount," the "Beatitudes" (Matthew 5:3-12) gives us each a barometer to test our heart's level of surrender to God. Ultimately, I believe spiritual healing is the deeper meaning of this passage. But as I struggled with my own family's health, I found this passage to be helpful for physical and emotional healing as well.

What seemed in the world's eyes to be tragedies—my bout with life-threatening cancer, our son's fight with leukemia and our daughter's chronic health issues—have actually been "upside-down" blessings to our family. We did not immediately see the blessings, but as we look back now, we can see that God led us through stages of faith and trust. Through these times, he enabled us to not only be stronger spiritually, but also physically and emotionally.

Jesus' truths are consistent truths at all levels of our existence: physical, mental, emotional and spiritual. His truths about the spiritual body (the church) and the physical human body mirror each other (1 Corinthians 12:12-31). Our mental and emotional states will influence our spiritual lives negatively unless we exercise self-control. "Therefore be clear minded and self-controlled so that you can pray" (1 Peter 4:7). On the other hand, our spiritual state influences our mental, emotional physical states. David clearly describes this connection:

> When I kept silent,
>   my bones wasted away
>   through my groaning all day long.
> For day and night
>   your hand was heavy upon me;
> my strength was sapped
>   as in the heat of summer.
> Then I acknowledged my sin to you
>   and did not cover up my iniquity.
> I said, "I will confess
>   my transgressions to the LORD"—
> and you forgave
>   the guilt of my sin.
>
> *Psalm 32:3-5*

I will leave it to others to discourse on this fascinating relationship between the condition of the soul and the condition of the body. I merely wish to share how using the principles in the Beatitudes helped me to victoriously face illness and pain time after time.

I am *blessed.* You can be, too!

10

The End of Self-Reliance

*"Blessed are the poor in spirit,
for theirs is the kingdom of heaven."*
Matthew 5:3

Helpless, futile, powerless, overwhelmed, shocked, fearful, debilitated, weak, desperate—words that describe how we feel when life's circumstances are totally beyond our control. When a mother's kiss can't take away the big hurts, when hugs are given but not felt, when words of comfort are spoken but not heard, when the devastation of the moment sends your spirit tailspinning into the vast void of numbness and into the whirlwind of panic, when you are humbled by your own inability to handle life, then you are on the threshold of being poor in spirit. So why does Jesus say that this is a blessed or happy state of affairs?

The Futility of Self-Reliance

Paul answers that question as he describes his hardships in 2 Corinthians 1:8-11: "We were under great pressure, far beyond our ability to endure, so that we despaired even of life" (v. 8). Ever been there? Did you like being there? Did you stay there for a long time? Paul didn't stay there. He searched deeply and prayed fervently for God to give him understanding during this challenging time. He concludes that "this happened that we might not rely on ourselves but on God, who raises the dead" (v. 9). On God, not self.

Self-reliance is spiritually stupid. But the fact that something is stupid never seems to stop humans from doing it. "Stupid is as stupid does," to quote the famous philosopher Forrest Gump. Jeremiah, the prophet, describes such stupidity and its consequences:

Cursed is the one who trusts in man,
   who depends on flesh for his strength
   and whose heart turns away from the Lord.
He will be like a bush in the wastelands;
   he will not see prosperity when it comes.

Jeremiah 17:5-6

Did you ever feel like a tumbleweed in a windstorm? I felt that way for years when I was not relying on God for my strength. It didn't even have to be a heavy wind; even a small breeze blew my emotions and fears all over the landscape. As I shared earlier, burnt toast used to set my day into a downward spiral. Then when life's challenges got to be light-years beyond my control, I began to get the big picture; I began to learn about trusting God. When the doctors told us that Michael had leukemia, I knew from experience that there was nothing I could do to fix it: My paternal grandfather died at age forty with leukemia. In high school, one of my friends' younger sisters died of leukemia. Our next door neighbor's little son had died the previous year of leukemia. What could *I* do to change anything? Only God could do something with this apparent tragedy.

Jeremiah went on to say:

But blessed is the man who trusts in the Lord,
   whose confidence is in him.
He will be like a tree planted by the water
   that sends out its roots by the stream.
It does not fear when heat comes;
   its leaves are always green.

Jeremiah 17:7-8

When my spiritual roots were drawing strength from me, from my husband or even from other godly people, I dried up. Only God, the source of love, can refill our empty reservoir. In fact, he can fill it to capacity with so much love and strength that we have plenty to give to others too. And he will continue to fill it up as long as we stay close to him.

To experience true physical, spiritual and emotional healing, we have to start by admitting, "I do not have the resources or ability to overcome on my own power. *I need God!"* The apostle Paul learned to "delight in weaknesses, in insults, in hardships, in persecutions, in difficulties" because he realized that "when I am weak, then I am strong" (2 Corinthians 12:10). When we can't, won't, don't or barely admit our weaknesses, God can't help us.

This reminds me of the time when I walked up to my then three-year-old daughter who was trying to yank her coat off our coat tree. I casually watched her struggle for a few moments, and then I offered, "I'm right here, honey. I would be glad to help you if you would just ask me." Yank, yank, yank. She continued her futile process. How many of us are trying to "yank down" our own problems when God could easily help us if we would just ask.

Knowing and Trusting God

On days that we do realize our own poverty of spirit, our lack of strength and wisdom, do we trust God? Not usually. Why not? Because we really don't know him. And when we don't know him, we don't know how rich in power and love he really is. We act as though he is as poor as we are. We have not taken time to look at his bank account. We forget that he actually *owns* the bank! Maybe we have the idea that God is as rich as Uncle Scrooge McDuck and just as greedy. God is neither powerless nor greedy. He wants us to individually realize our need for him so that we will come to him for the very help only he can give.

Jesus' good friend Peter tells us that "through our knowledge of God...we can have all that we need for life and godliness" (2 Peter 1:3-4). Did you hear that? If we know God—not just a *feeling,* but a relationship—he will meet all of our needs.

Are you like me? I like the shortcuts to knowledge, the *Reader's Digest* condensed version of life. True knowledge takes time to gather. However, over the years I have found some treasured scriptures that quickened the "enlightening" process for me. John, the disciple with whom Jesus had a special bond of love, discourses on the truth that "God is love" in 1 John 4:7-21. Therefore, to know God is to know love.

Paul's description of love in 1 Corinthians 13:4-8 is also a vivid description of God's character. Read through the chapter inserting "God" wherever the word "love" appears, and come face to face with the very heart of God. This is he who loves you and who loves me. Who could not totally trust someone who is the perfection of all these qualities?

Not only has God tried to tell us who he is through the written Word, but he put on skin and walked the earth: Jesus is love with skin on it. We learn about his capacity to love by reading about his sacrificial life in the gospels. We see him cry over Jerusalem. We see him touch the "untouchable" with healing compassion. We watch him carry his cross to Golgotha and witness the full extent of his love as he is suspended between the heaven he left and the earth he came to save.

The truth is, God loves us. But sometimes, as rational, reasonable, intelligent, responsible (and prideful) people, we allow our own reasoning to get in the way of truth. In fact, at every moment spiritual warfare is going on in our minds: our reasoning versus God's reasoning. Paul describes the spiritual warfare being waged for the life and soul of the Corinthian church in 2 Corinthians 10:3-5:

> For though we live in the world, we do not wage war as the world does. The weapons we fight with are not the weapons of the world. On the contrary, they have divine power to demolish strongholds. We demolish arguments and every pretension that sets itself up against the knowledge of God, and we take captive every thought to make it obedient to Christ.

Although he is talking about a struggle with unspiritual people who opposed his leadership and cast doubt on his apostleship, there is a model here that applies very well to the internal battles in our own lives.

God's knowledge is trying to reach our hearts and minds, but it has to first break through several barricades that we put up. First are the "strongholds," which can be the parts of our character that we find the most difficult to change. These well-fortified areas are where our old natures dig in and take their final stand. These strongholds include thick walls designed to protect the old self. We hide behind walls out of our fear of being vulnerable and weak.

Second, we allow "arguments"—wrong thoughts and lies about God's nature—to keep us from being close to God. These barriers come from Satan himself, from the enemy. If he can get us to believe that God doesn't really love us, for instance, he can keep us from knowing God. If he causes us to think that there are areas in our lives that we can never change, he can keep us from knowing God. These thoughts set themselves "up against the knowledge of God" in our hearts. And, again, if we do not know him, we will not trust him. Whichever argument works on whichever person, he will use it to keep us from knowing our God.

Finally, from our lofty towers of pride and "pretension," we look down on and try to eliminate any truth that might make us look foolish or wrong. *Stop it! Give up!* Wave the white flag. Admit that you are afraid, weak, faithless, foolish and prideful, and surrender your thoughts to God so that he can reform them. As Paul told the Romans,

> Do not conform any longer to the pattern of this world, but be transformed by the renewing of your mind. Then you will be able to test and approve what God's will is—his good, pleasing and perfect will.
>
> *Romans 12:2*

Suffering punctuates the reality of our own limits. That's why God calls suffering a blessed place to be in life: It is one place where we truly realize our need for God. In fact, it may be the only place where many of us will finally decide to trust the One who has infinitely more power and wisdom than we do. *It is often in suffering that we finally allow him to do his work in our lives.*

Therefore, the first step of God's healing process is followed by a statement of hope. To those who are willing to admit their own weakness and to rely on God, he says, "The kingdom of heaven is yours!"

11

Grief That Really Is Good

"Blessed are those who mourn,
for they will be comforted."

Matthew 5:4

We go to great lengths to avoid hurt, sadness, pain and mourning. We spend time, energy and money dulling or heading off anything unpleasant. If we get hurt, we carry personal "comfort bags" to give ourselves a quick fix of happiness. What do people carry in their comfort bags? Food, cigarettes, money, charge cards, pills, M&Ms, a flask? If we experience some emotional pain, we busy ourselves with compulsive behaviors to numb the sadness (chocoholics, workaholics, work-our-bodies, etc.). We collectively spend millions of dollars on health spas, vacations, getaways and building and redecorating projects to hide us from pain. We pay professionals to try to fix us when we hurt. If we can't afford a professional, we find someone to share our misery. Deny it, drown it out, run away from it and salve the symptoms, but try as hard as we may to avoid it, at some point, trouble and hurt will catch up with us, and we will have to deal with it.

Since no one likes to mourn, why would Jesus call it a blessed state? Did he have one of those twisted minds that relishes pain and anguish? Not at all. He just understood how needed it often is in getting us from where we are to where we need to be.

Jesus knew that when we mourn *with faith* it will lead to comfort, and as I have seen, that means more than just "relief." It means something better and richer than I had before. Many times we try to avoid the grief because we do not believe that we will be comforted. Or else we are not fully confident that mourning is an acceptable thing for a Christian to do. I believe that God wants us to understand the necessity and the benefits of true mourning.

Spiritual Mourning

Jesus' primary meaning in the context of the Beatitudes was surely that we should mourn *over our sin*. James (whose writings contain many allusions to the Sermon on the Mount) tells us about the role grief plays in spiritual healing:

> Come near to God and he will come near to you. Wash you hands, you sinners, and purify your hearts, you double-minded. Grieve, mourn and wail. Change your laughter to mourning and your joy to gloom. Humble yourselves before the Lord, and he will lift you up.
>
> *James 4:8-10*

We must have a godly sorrow for our sin. Just feeling bad about sin will not result in lasting change or forgiveness from God, the one who sees our true hearts (2 Corinthians 7:8-12). We must be hurt by realizing the pain that our sin causes God in order for us to be comforted by the amazing extent of his forgiveness. There is simply no painless way to come to God. If we do not mourn, we will not know him.[1]

If this kind of mourning leads to such a healthy outcome in our relationship with God, we can assume that the principle would find powerful applications in other areas. It is on these other types of mourning that I will focus this chapter.

Mourning or Moaning?

The Bible contains numerous references to people mourning. When Lazarus died and was in the tomb, Jesus wept (John 11:35). David grieved for days over the imminent death of his infant son (2 Samuel 12:15-23). Ecclesiastes 3:4 says that there is a time to mourn and a time to dance. Examples in the Old Testament even indicate that it takes time to mourn (Genesis 50:4, 11).

The definition of "mourn" is "to feel or express lament; to

grieve." To "lament" is to cry out in grief or to wail. We mourn significant losses—not only the death of a loved one, but also a critical illness or disability in our life or the life of someone we love. The loss of a job or a relationship or anything else meaningful to us may also be an occasion to mourn.

Some losses are significant enough to necessitate grieving before being able to proceed toward the healing of God's comfort. But there is a difference between mourning and *moaning.* If we don't know the difference, that could explain the lack of comfort that we are receiving. Moaning reaps negative responses from God and from those around us because moaning is centered in self-pity and faithlessness. Moaning broadcasts the message, "I feel hopeless, and don't try to change my mind."

Before I perceived my pattern of self-pity and moaning, Roger used to ask me, "Do you enjoy being miserable?"

After dusting off my sackcloth and ashes one day, I decided to investigate that "insensitive" comment, biblically! Sure enough, there it was. Jesus basically asked the invalid by the pool of Bethesda the same question, "Do you want to get well?" (John 5:1-15). At first I thought, *That's obvious, isn't it? Of course he wanted to get well.* After thinking a few minutes, I began to wonder, *Did he, really?* Since then, Jesus' words have penetrated the stiffness of my paralyzed faith. Do I really want to get well, or am I happy just moaning about my problems? Do I impede my healing with thoughts such as these: *If I get well, then I might not get any attention. If I get well, someone might expect me to take on more responsibility and that sounds like hard work. If I get well, someone might not remember that I used to be sick, and they might expect too much out of me.*

Mourning will bring sorrow for a period of time, but a moaning spirit brings sorrow for a lifetime.

It's Okay to Mourn

On the other hand, getting hardened, numb or pulling ourselves up by our own bootstraps—a.k.a. pride—is not, as it may seem, the opposite of self-pity. Both attitudes are very self-protecting. Anyone who chooses either attitude does not trust God's protection and comfort.

When cancer hit our family for the second time, this time in me, we all tried hard to be brave for one another. A close family friend came by to visit us one day. After spending some time with us, she began to cry. "Why are you crying?" I asked.

"It's because you are all hurting so much," she said.

"No we're not," I quipped. "We're coping just fine."

But she saw past our stoic faces. Her honesty helped us to be real. And when I got real, I had to admit that everyone's brave front made me feel as though no one would miss me if I did die. Our stoic bravery was sealing off emotions that should have been expressed to each other.

When I learned to let myself mourn losses, my hurts healed more quickly. When we moved to California and left our twenty-year-old daughter in school in Massachusetts, I tried to be brave and stoic about the whole thing until I told myself, "No, this hurts to leave her. I am going to let myself feel the hurt, cry and then move on."

After I was given the news of Michael's congestive heart failure (discussed in Chapter 7), I wailed and cried for about thirty minutes. I prayed and had an open talk with God about how I was feeling. I struggled with feeling that it was just not fair after all he had been through. But because I allowed myself time to work through it, I was able to handle Michael's sorrow with more strength and confidence in God. When I suppress my sorrow, it can come out in very inappropriate ways.

Now I can allow others to mourn both because of knowing my own need to be comforted and because I have seen the need in others. I counseled a young woman once who had great difficulty emotionally trusting God. She perceived him as uncaring and harsh. I asked her about her past, and she told me of the tragedy she experienced as a young child: Both her parents died within a month of each other, and of course, the sorrow was overwhelming to her. She and her sisters moved in with their aunt, uncle and four cousins. In their new home the children were not allowed to grieve. Their aunt matter-of-factly related to them how their lives would change from that point on. No one hugged or comforted the recently orphaned children. They were not allowed to have pictures of their parents. Even mentioning their parents was forbidden, so the girls had to sneak off together to cry and talk about them. She could not understand how God could let her be in so much pain.

After studying the characteristics of God in the Bible, she began to understand that since God is love (1 John 4:16), his character is revealed in 1 Corinthians 13: 4-6 (more on this in Chapter 10). She became convinced that the way she was treated after the death of her parents was not God's way. She realized that he must have been sad too. Her heart softened toward God and she finally mourned her loss and trusted in God's comforting. Later that year, she married a wonderful man and became "Mother" to his daughter. The special irony was that his daughter was the same age she had been when she lost her parents. She wholeheartedly wanted to love and cherish her new daughter in the way she had newly discovered that God loved and cherished her.

Medical and psychological research shows that those who grieve go through certain stages. These stages are: denial, isolation, anger, blaming, bargaining, depression and finally, acceptance. Have you known someone who is stuck in one of these stages after a great loss? When we, as disciples, allow ourselves to mourn, we will still go through some or all of these stages to some extent, but we will *get through* them with God's help and comfort. If we do not allow ourselves or others to mourn, we are putting off the inevitable and setting up ourselves and others for misery.

Our experience with Michael's leukemia diagnosis taught us that people will work through their grief in different ways. I was the emotional "let's-just-sit-and-hold-each-other" type of mourner and Roger was the "fixer-upper" mourner. If he could be sure that the car was fixed, the insurance was paid

and all the medical records were in order, etc., then he felt
better about things. We each thought the other was not handling this trauma "properly" until we realized that we each
handled mourning differently. There is no proper protocol.
Roger felt the need to be the strong leader who held us all
together. I learned later that he had been crying in the shower
every morning; whereas I cried everywhere else.

Children have a different method of working through their
grief. Because it is difficult for them to verbalize their feelings,
they often play them out. I heard this in a child development
course in college, but my firsthand experience with it came
while I was a live-in baby-sitter. The boys' mother had gone to
the hospital for surgery. Due to complications, she was in the
hospital weeks longer than expected. Every day her children
played hospital. I had to be the patient. Every day I had to
reassure them that I was getting better and better. After the
first week of playing hospital, their father told me that their
grandmother had gone into the hospital and had never come
back home. She had died there. The boys' behavior made perfect sense to me once I understood what had happened in their
past.

My son Michael gave all his toys bone marrow extractions,
spinal taps, shots and medicine. Everything had a Band-Aid
on it!

Children can also use drawing to express their feelings.
Michael did a lot of "good soldier" blood cell and "bad soldier" cancer cell drawings. The good soldiers always won, of
course, because those cells were on God's side. To try to understand how Michael was feeling, I would ask him questions
like; "What pictures are in your mind now?" "What is the best
thing that happened to you today?" "What is the worst thing
that happened today?" Sometimes I would have to start a conversation by saying, "When I was six years old, if I had to go to
the doctor every Friday for 'finger sticks,' I might be thinking
that I have so many holes in me that all the water I drink will
spill out the holes." That would get Michael to express bad
things with "silly words" that finally progressed to more seri-

ous thoughts. This also helped his sister, Christie, and his brother, David, to understand how Michael was feeling and to empathize.

We would all probably be healthier emotionally if we tried some type of "play therapy" to work through our grief. Our neighbors, Stan and Jan McMorris, tried to relieve Shane's fear of spinal taps by putting on straw hats, carrying canes and tap dancing down the hall on the way to having his procedure done.

Shane's younger brother, Kelly, was David's best friend. After Shane died and Michael was diagnosed with leukemia, I began to notice that David and Kelly dressed up and played "super heroes" all the time. David seldom went to preschool dressed as an ordinary kid; he was Popeye, the Hulk, Superman, a football hero or Luke Skywalker. Reflecting on those days, I now wonder if David and Kelly had to be super heroes to cope with their feelings of helplessness against the "enemy powers" attacking their families.

Mourn with Those Who Mourn

Once we have been comforted by God, we will know how to comfort others (2 Corinthians 1:3-7). Again, we must first let ourselves feel the hurt so that we can feel the comfort. I am convinced that most of us do not allow ourselves or our children to feel discomfort, much less sorrow, enough. We have become callous people who raise callous children. This was brought to my attention when I worked in a preschool in Sudbury, Massachusetts. The head teacher, Janet Hammonds, is a disciple of Jesus who uses godly principles in her classroom. When one child hurt another child, she would bring the two together for reconciliation. Before she asked for apologies, she would tell the child who had done the hitting or hurting, "Look at your friend's face. See his tears. See how much he is hurting." By this time the hitter is squirming to get away until she says, "Do you remember a time when you were hurt like that? Remember how bad you felt?" Even as she got the words out, apologies were being made and hugs were being given. It's amazing how shared sorrow increases our capacity to empathize, love and reconcile.

Romans 12:15 encourages us to "mourn with those who mourn." I was told once, "A joy shared is multiplied. A sorrow shared is divided." Similarly, the apostle Paul exhorts us to take the comfort that we have been given and give it to others. The people who were able to offer the most comfort to our family and to me personally were people who had suffered similar losses. I felt an immediate bond with widows and others to whom I had not related before.

Let Go

Occasionally, people need to "let go" in order to reach the acceptance stage of grief. When Shane died of leukemia, one of the family friends took his death especially hard. The last time that she had seen Shane, he was hooked up to tubes and wires to support his little dying body. In an effort to let go of those painful memories, she went to his grave site and released helium balloons. As she let the strings slip through her fingers, she imagined Shane being released to be with God.

For those who choose to trust God, mourning does eventually lead to letting go—letting go of how things could or should have been and accepting things as they now are, surrendering to God again.

The Source of All Comfort

There will come a time when *only* God can give the comfort that we need. When Jesus went to the garden, he prayed in deep sorrow before facing the cross. He had asked his closest friends to be with him. They had come, but then they emotionally deserted him by sleeping through his pain. Luke 22:45 says that they were asleep because they were "exhausted from sorrow." Jesus' only source of strength at that time was God (Psalm 16). We may feel deserted by friends and family at our greatest hour of need. Our isolation may actually be due to their own sorrow. Friends may be hurting so bad that they do not know what to say. Their own lack of personal sorrow may keep them from relating to our level of grief. Others may leave us alone out of a fear of association with sorrow. No matter where our friends are emotionally, God is always there. He promises never to leave us. Only he can give us the "peace which transcends all understanding" (Philippians 4:7).

We must fully mourn, and then let God fully comfort us.

12

Humble and Happy

"Blessed are the meek,
for they will inherit the earth."
Matthew 5:5

Meekness: the Key to Success is not the title found on today's best-seller list. Yet, Jesus says that the meek will inherit the earth. He also says that the meek will be blessed with a happiness that is not dependent upon circumstances. To most of us, meekness implies weakness, but God gives us a very different definition in the Scripture.

Humble Before God

God likes to illustrate his lessons in human form. Moses was called the "most humble" (or "meekest" in KJV) man on earth (Numbers 12:3). By the time Moses led the children of Israel out of Egypt, he had learned to humbly accept God's authority and lordship in his life. Through the years he had come to know God; he had come to have a deep friendship with him. And coming to know God had caused Moses to trust him.

Ignorance of God and his character leads to personal arrogance on our part. We are arrogant when we trust ourselves instead of trusting God. In his book, *The Victory of Surrender,* Gordon Ferguson powerfully develops the theme of meekness as surrender to God. He explores surrender as our key to spiritual success. He also beautifully reveals the God to whom we surrender. Without a clear view of God, meekness and surrender would be out of the question.[1]

While still in Egypt, Moses saw the oppression of his people and wanted desperately to make a difference. But rather than trusting God, he relied on himself. He reacted to the cruelty of an Egyptian by killing him. Like Moses, many of us aggressively seek to make a difference in this world. In pursuit of our dreams, we find weakness unacceptable and so we reason "meekness" is also out of the question. God certainly needs bold people, but we need to be bold for him in his chosen way.

As I shared earlier, our daughter, Christie, was a dynamic teenager when she was hit with Chronic Fatigue Syndrome, fibromyalgia and endometriosis. She has always had a very strong character; she has admittedly tried to take charge of practically everything since birth! God had a plan to refine and use her strengths, but he had to first get her attention—as he must with all of us. Let me share with you Christie's own words:

> No one wants to consider themselves weak—especially when they have a strong self-will and character. I was very confident in my future goals and dreams. I wanted to be a top leader as a teen who would then go to a top university, graduate in four years and then go right into a full-time ministry position in a campus or teen ministry. I knew I had leadership strengths, and I was very confident in them. But I had forgotten why I became a disciple of Jesus.
>
> It took God's discipline to show me that my heart was not right. The heart of what Jesus' ministry and spiritual leadership is all about is loving people more than yourself, serving and not caring about your own personal status. God taught me that being meek in the Lord is a godly characteristic and not a weak or wimpy one, as I had once thought. He taught me to rely on him for my strength. Being *meek* is being *strong* in the Lord and in his mighty power.

After seven long years of struggling with her health, Christie has recently seen incredible improvement, and she is now working full-time in campus ministry. She did get the desires of her heart after God refined her. I pondered many times why she had not learned these lessons about meekness from Roger and me as we had been through so many struggles. But God knows what experiences each of us individually needs, and he graciously gives us private tutoring!

God definitely knew exactly what Moses needed: Forty years of tending his father-in-law's sheep taught Moses to be meek and useful to God. And it took forty years of wandering in the desert for the children of Israel to learn meekness. Chronic illness can seem like forty years in the desert; it, too, will teach us to rely on God if we allow it to.

Content, but Not Complacent

Moses had once been the powerful son of Pharaoh's daughter with authority and influence, but suddenly he was "demoted" to God's school of shepherding. When illness comes into our lives, we may feel like we have been demoted, especially when our normal load of responsibility is lightened. Little did Moses know that while he was taking care of the sheep, God was preparing him to shepherd millions of people. He must have struggled with his pride and arrogance as he thought of how his talents and princely experiences were being wasted on sheep. And there was no one to cheer his meager efforts except God. Similarly, there will be times that our physical limitations may make our spiritual efforts seem pitifully meager. Then we just have to trust God and take a lesson from the widow who gave God her only two small coins—she gave all that she had, and God was pleased (Luke 21:2-4).

After learning to be content as a lowly shepherd, God knew Moses was ready to be called to a bigger challenge. However, Moses had begun to feel comfortable and safe leading sheep and wasn't so sure that he wanted to lead millions of people. He had lost confidence in his own abilities to speak or influence anyone. He was finally where God wanted him. As a humbled man, he would now be ready to see the power of God.

Getting comfortable and lazy in our lowly state is a great temptation when we are sick. A couple of years after my surgery, I clearly remember going to the beach with my family. It was a hot summer day, yet I was sitting all bound up in a blanket, hat and sweat suit. Everyone else was running back and forth to the ocean, carefree and warm. I wondered, *Why am I so cold and fearful?* I began to see how I had gotten so self-protective that I was right back where I started before I gave my life over to God many years earlier. I had begun to put up my shell of self-protection and fear again.

When I became a disciple, I had decided to shed my shell and entrust my whole life to God. God had made my life and spirit abundant and free, but now, using the excuse that I was "sickly," I became burdened again, focusing on all my limitations and tenaciously protecting myself from stress or death. Feeling the spiritual death-grip of Satan, I decided, *Short-lived or long, God is going to have the controls again. I am not afraid to die because God saved me from eternal punishment; therefore, I am not going to be afraid to live radically for him. I do have physical limits, but my heart, faith and love will be his without limits.*

Moses may have been commended by God as a meek man, but we see that his meekness caused him to be very bold. He expected the Israelites to be obedient to God. He made bold moves to get them to understand God's righteous laws. Of course, not all the people accepted God as their authority—even though they were God's chosen people. In the same way, many people today who call themselves Christians do not accept the lordship of Jesus or the authority of his word. Some acknowledge allegiance to God intellectually, but not in *every* life circumstance. They make exceptions to their obedience due to personal circumstances. Those of us with physical challenges are especially prone to the temptation to make ourselves the "exception" to obedience. But God does not make exceptions to seeking first the kingdom of God and his righteousness (Matthew 6:33).

On the other hand, God does not ask the impossible. He gives us what we need to obey him. God gave Moses help with speaking by having his brother Aaron speak for him at first. And he used the rod in Moses' hand to do miracles. Just as with Moses, God will probably not give us *new* abilities and strengths (new bodies, new legs, etc.), but he will work with us, help us build our faith and mold us until we are suited for his purposes. "For we are *God's workmanship*, created in Christ

Jesus to do good works, which God prepared in advance for us to do" (Ephesians 2:10, emphasis added).

Meekness does not mean we are helpless and hopeless. God wants us to be surrendered to his control, but that does not mean we give up on life and become victims of our bodies or our circumstances. In order to achieve health or the ability to function, we must also be an active participant in the healing process—whatever form that healing may take. In many healings that Jesus performed, he expected the person to do something. Those he healed were directed to do various things: "Get up, take your mat and walk," "Go wash [your eyes]," or "Go show yourself to the priest and offer the sacrifices." They demonstrated humble, obedient and surrendered hearts by their actions. The result was a healing. On the other hand, sitting and waiting for something to happen to us is false faith and shows little understanding of God's ways.

Get Advice

God gives us wise counselors, physicians and spiritual leaders to help us. In order to make the most of the help we are given, we have to first admit our limitations, then get help and advice, and finally, work within our limitations. A woman who has been a great guide and help in my life is Patricia Gempel. Pat and her husband, Bob, oversee the entire operation of HOPE Worldwide, a benevolent organization that helps the sick and needy through more than seventy projects worldwide. She had the opportunity to speak at the Fourth Annual World Conference on Women in Beijing in 1995. I respect and admire Pat in all areas of her life. She is the consummate "Proverbs 31 woman." She is a woman of spiritual wisdom, energy and excellent knowledge of the health care field.

When my health collapsed in 1987, I needed Pat's perspective to help me figure out when to push my body and when to rest. She told Roger to observe me for a while to see how much sleep and rest I needed to function best. We discovered that without adequate rest I would experience mental confusion, forgetfulness and irrational emotions before my body would even feel fatigued. As a result of his observations, we decided that I needed a nap daily and that I should have no expectations put on me between 10 p.m. and 10 a.m. On days when I didn't *feel* tired, I wanted to resist napping and going to bed early like a little kid. But, in time I realized the wisdom of the advice.

Yes, there were many times that the needs of the moment or the needs of people around me took priority over my rest. Those were the days that I felt God's Spirit working to make up for what I personally lacked. However, overall, taking their advice has given me renewed mental and physical strength. Meekness means getting advice and then following it.

Since the Bible refers to our body as God's temple, we each need to actively maintain it in a way that honors God. Our bodies are important to God, and he expects us to use our heads and discipline ourselves to take the best care of them possible. Paul wrote,

> Do you not know that your body is a temple of the Holy Spirit, who is in you, whom you have received from God? You are not your own; you were bought at a price. Therefore honor God with your body.
>
> *1 Corinthians 6:19*

Jars of Clay

God also illustrates meekness on the potter's wheel. We are like clay being shaped and molded by God's hands for God's purposes (Isaiah 64:8). It is important that clay be meek. God shows us the foolishness of clay thinking it is the potter in passages like Romans 9:20-21:

> But who are you, O man to talk back to God? "Shall what is formed say to him who formed it, 'Why did you make me like this?'" Does not the potter have the right to make out of the same lump of clay some pottery for noble purposes and some for common use?

It is unthinkable, and yet we are quick to tell God how he

has messed up our lives. Just spend a moment thinking about the process of pottery. In order to get to the goal of a beautiful or useful vessel, the clay has to be put through some uncomfortable positions. It can't even be worked with unless it is softened with a punch here and there and a good dousing with water. Imagine clay refusing to be moved by the potter.

God has his way of dealing with the really hard clay; it is called breaking and crushing. Do you ever wonder why "bad things happen to good clay"? Or why we have to face the fiery furnace just when we have surrendered and become obedient, trusting clay? Molding the form is just the beginning. To set it, strengthen it, and to burn out any impurities, it must be put into a fiery kiln. It is a painful process, but it is necessary. The outcome brings glory to God, the potter. You may ask after all this, "Why does he need us pots anyway?" The answer is simple: He keeps his treasure in us (2 Corinthians 4:7).

This lesson of the potter and the clay was vividly placed in my heart during Michael's treatments for leukemia. One Sunday the sermon was on Isaiah 64:8. Our campus minister, Andy Van Buren, used that text to illustrate our need to trust God and be vulnerable to his plans.

That afternoon I took a rare break and visited an arts-and-crafts show at the Eastern Illinois University campus. Still trying to piece together what was happening to Michael and to us, I walked through the displays in a bit of a dazed state. Suddenly, a pottery display caught my eye. Among the jars was a beautiful crockery jar engraved with Isaiah 64:8, "Yet, O Lord, you are our Father. We are the clay, you are the potter; we are all the work of your hand." Sitting on top of the jar was a little clay potter at his wheel making a clay pot. I was stunned.

Talking to the artist, I learned that he was suffering from Cystic Fibrosis and made his living as a potter. He told me he had recently come to believe in God, and this was his way of sharing his faith, even though he felt very unfamiliar with the Bible. When I found out that he was from DeKalb, Illinois, I asked him if he would like me to give his name and number to my friend, Marty Fuqua, who was a campus minister at Northern Illinois University at the time. He wholeheartedly agreed.

Several months later, I received a "birth announcement" in the mail. Not only had *he* been baptized into Christ, but his wife had too. Before the craft show at EIU the next year, I received a phone call from my new brother in Christ, Mark Gubleman, saying he wanted me to come by his booth to say hi. I was thrilled to see him, and even more thrilled when he handed me a gift—the Isaiah 64 jar. It still holds "treasured" memories of God's molding of my faith.[2]

God Always in Control

God is wholly capable and qualified to be in control of every aspect of our lives. This is why it always makes sense to yield to him. He created us. He knows how we work. He knows the most fulfilling way for us to live. Yet, in our simple human reasoning, we think that some things are beyond his control. (Perhaps the only thing that is beyond his control is our decision to trust him, but he even does everything in his power to get us to do that.) We tend to pigeonhole certain areas of our lives as impossible places for the work of God. Until I read Psalm 139 I hated to be anesthetized for surgery because I couldn't be alert and "in control." David expresses the infinite knowledge that God has of you and me. Verses 13-16 describe his knowledge of our conception and development:

> For you created my inmost being;
>> you knit me together in my mother's womb.
> I praise you because I am fearfully and wonderfully made;
>> your works are wonderful,
>> I know that full well.
> My frame was not hidden from you
>> when I was made in the secret place.
> When I was woven together in the depths of the earth,
>> your eyes saw my unformed body.
> All the days ordained for me
>> were written in your book
>> before one of them came to be.

This Psalm expands our faith by explaining to us that God always is aware of where and how we are, even when we are not aware. Even in the darkest moments of our lives or the darkness of anesthetized surgery, God is there. Verses 11-12 assure us of his presence:

> If I say, "Surely, the darkness will hide me
>   and the light become night around me,"
> even the darkness will not be dark to you;
>   the night will shine like the day
>   for darkness is as light to you.

Just because we are not in control and everything is darkness around us doesn't mean that it is darkness to God. Truth is truth in the darkness or the light.

Bridled Emotions

Meekness can be defined as "controlled strength." The word Jesus uses in the Beatitudes is the same word used to describe a powerful stallion once it is broken and under control. Just as reigns in the hands of a trainer control the strength of a horse, we have strength that needs to be put under God's control to be effective in our lives.

God has given us, as human beings, the strength of emotions. When surrendered to God, emotions can be channeled to help our healing process. But if they are left "unbridled" they can make our condition worse.

Unbridled crying sometimes helps if it is a part of our mourning a loss, but many of us, especially women, are guilty of gushing so much that we don't think our tears can be bridled. I believe tears are God-given. Some days a good cry can clean the cobwebs out of our emotional gears and get things running smoothly again. (Trust me, men, this is when you just hold that woman and say, "It will be all right!" No sermonettes, please.) But there is "a time to weep and a time to laugh" (Ecclesiastes 3:4). Unbridled weeping that stems from self-pity is destructive and useless. A constant self-focus will warp our view of the world, blind us to God's help and others' need for our help.

On the third day of Michael's initial hospital stay, I was overcome with crying. I couldn't seem to stop myself. Realizing that this was having a negative effect on young Michael, I left him in the nurses' care for a few minutes while I went out to pray. I prayed that God would help me to be strong for Michael's sake, and I prayed that God would keep me from getting totally caught up in my own sorrow. God's answer came quickly.

When I returned to the room, Michael was peacefully asleep. At first I thought that God was giving me the opportunity to cry freely until an unexpected visitor arrived. I had never met this man before, but he was a ministry friend of Roger's. In the course of our conversation, I realized that he was spiritually hurting. We talked for a long time, and I shared with him how God had helped us spiritually over the past few years. Then he prayed for Michael and as he left, he thanked me for giving him hope. To my amazement, God used this man's need for encouragement for my encouragement as well! God put my eyes outward beyond my sorrow to comfort another.

Two emotions we must bridle are fear and anger.

Bridled Fear

Being brave in the midst of chaos and turmoil takes a deep trust in God. We must build on the foundation of being "poor in spirit," "mourned and comforted," and developing a "meekness before God" before we can subdue these wild emotions. We fear what we cannot control. Critical illness is usually something out of our control.

Fear is the opposite of trust and love. John says in 1 John 4:18 that "perfect love drives out fear," so, the only way to combat fear is to attack it with great love. Our great love for Michael enabled us to face years of frightening procedures. Our increasing love for God helped us to overcome other personal fears.

Not surprisingly, Michael had developed a tremendous fear of shots and other medical treatments. During a regular grade-school physical exam, Michael needed to get his immunizations updated. His dread and fear of this event began to escalate to hurricane proportions. Two nurses and the doctor had to hold him down. Nothing could ease his panic. Finally, after the wrestling match was over and the shot was given, I tried, again, to reason with Michael and understand what triggered his panic. "What scares you so much, Michael? Is it the shots?"

"No Mom, I've had lots of shots," said Michael.

"Is it the pain?" I quizzed.

"No, Mom, the pain is not that bad," he said.

"Then what?" I begged.

"It's me, Mom, I'm afraid of me and how I am when I get like this [out of control emotionally]," he cried. "It always happens to me."

He pinpointed a fear that many of us cannot verbalize or identify—the fear of ourselves.

One reason we cannot always identify fear is because fear does not always appear as shaky knees, chattering teeth and a rapid pulse. Fear can come disguised as rebellion, agitation, anger, irresponsibility, aloofness and frustration.

Often, on the day before Michael's trips to St. Louis Children's hospital for his monthly bone marrow and spinal tests, he and I found ourselves nit-picking and arguing with each other. To an onlooker, it would seem as if we were angry with each other. So, one morning instead of being our usual irritable selves, I sat Michael down, and we talked. "You know, Michael," I said, "I am not angry at you for anything. I think I'm really just feeling scared. I don't like that you have to go through the pain of your tests and treatments. Frankly, I feel scared for you and me."

Michael quickly agreed, "I'm not angry either, Mom. I'm scared too."

We hugged, cried and prayed. The enemy was defined, we could fight it now with God's arsenal of truth.

After learning this important lesson, I was able to better identify the fear behind many of my reactions—and even

Roger's frustration. When I knew that it was fear that I was dealing with, I could respond more appropriately. Thinking that one of us, for some unknown reason, was angry had confused the real issue.

Fear can motivate us to do the right thing, but unchecked fear can lead us into sinful actions. (Think of all the irrational acts of violence that are sparked by uncontrolled fear.) How do we take control of this overpowering feeling? Knowing the source of fear helps us to combat it.

If God is wanting to fill us with faith (Mark 11:22) and self-control (Galatians 5:23), then the source of fear and panic must be our enemy, the devil. I have heard it said that fear is contagious and that the biggest coward of all is Satan. He rightfully is afraid because his doom is set. Therefore, when we feel fearful, Satan is lurking around. If he can get us caught up in his panic, then we will lose sight of God's power and love.[3] We combat his tactics with actions of love and faith. For example, during frightening medical procedures, we can combat Satan's attacks by loving our doctors and nurses and showing an interest in their spiritual well-being.

When we, as disciples, reach the point that we cannot control ourselves, God's Spirit can become more evident in our lives. With God's Spirit in us, we are given "a spirit of power, love and self-control" (2 Timothy 1:7, RSV). This self-control is not self-willed—it is God-given. We must be meek before God and admit our need for his strength and courage, and then boldly face our fears.

Bridled Anger

Anger unbridled will lash out at God and the very people trying to help us. When Michael first got leukemia, we got advice—lots of advice. Some of the advice sounded as though it came from Job's friends who were probing and trying to figure out why all the calamity came upon Job. (See Job chapters 2 through 31.) Their humanistic philosophizing sounded good on the surface, but it revealed their gross lack of knowledge of God's character. For example, the worst advice we got was to "get angry with God. Yell and scream at him. Tell him how unfair this is." Fortunately, we chose not to take that advice because God is not the enemy—Satan is. God is the "rescuer." He can make something good out of the worst situations (Romans 8:28).

We knew that we had been enemies of God (Romans 5:6-11), but even at our worst, God loved us enough to let his Son die for us. Our relationship with God was healed through Jesus' sacrifice. Anger at God was unreasonable at this point. However, later, during my bout with cancer, my heart was tested and revealed. I *was* capable of being angry with God (see Chapter 14). Roger gave us a great perspective on the unfairness of life when he said, "When I am tempted to think 'Why me?' I always have to ask, 'Why not me?'"

Children and adults can use anger when they feel that their freedom of choice or ability to be in control is taken away from them. Children will try to take control of a situation with fits of rage or stubborn rebellion. Taking away as much of their fear and oppression as possible is important. Many children at the clinic were allowed to administer their own medication after the nurse injected the needle to give them a little bit of "control" in the situation. Allowing them to make choices when possible helps them to feel respected (e.g. "Which arm do you want me to put your medicine in?").

Giving children a choice when there is no real choice is dishonest and will only create more anger and hostility (e.g. "Do you want a shot today?"). Changing phrases to less adversarial directions like, "I need you to hop up on the examining table" causes the child to think, *The poor guy needs my help.* This gives the child more incentive to be cooperative. If he is told, "You need to hop up on the examining table," he may rebelliously think, *You can't make me.*

Unfortunately, some of us still think and act like children when it comes to taking our doctor's direction and advice. In our anger over the inconvenience of illness and mortality we can childishly refuse to cooperate. This response is destructive both spiritually and physically. We need to pray for God's power to bridle such harmful emotions as this and meekly accept that help.

One of the greatest blessings that I realized from our tragic experiences is the blessing of seeing my continual need to rely on God through prayer and to gratefully obey his word every day. I have seen the blessing of God's solid truths that keep my helter-skelter emotions reined in. I have seen God's skillful hands work in my life and in the lives of those in my family. What started out as a heap of clay, God has refined and shaped for his great purpose! The challenge and privilege is to stay contentedly on the potter's wheel every day. As long as I remember to trust the potter, I can do that. God truly blesses the meek.

13

Real Satisfaction

"Blessed are those who hunger
and thirst for righteousness,
for they will be filled."

Matthew 5:6

There is still enough fringe on my Pharisaic robes to ask God questions like, "What do you mean by 'righteousness'?" "Just how much must I do to be righteous?" "Give me a specific measure of righteousness." In my search through concordances and commentaries for "righteousness" I came away with stained-glassed words such as "justification" and "redemption." Then when I read that righteousness is "summarily comprehended in the decalogue," I all but gave up. How can I hunger and thirst for righteousness if I don't even know what it is?

Thankfully, God led me to read a profound essay on righteousness, "Religious or Righteous?" by Fred Faller.[1] He shed new light on the meaning of this illusive word:

> To think like an Old Testament Jew one had to understand that even two thieves could be considered "righteous" in their relationship to one another if it was characterized by sharing, fairness, camaraderie and loyalty.
>
> Righteousness as it is understood in the OT is a thoroughly Hebraic concept, foreign to the Western mind and at variance with the common understanding of the term. The failure to understand its meaning is perhaps most responsible for the view of the OT religion as "legalistic" and as far removed from the graciousness of the NT.
>
> Rather, righteousness is, in the Old Testament, the fulfillment of the demands of a relationship, whether that relationship be with men or with God...
>
> Jesus saw that right relationships were the key to righteousness rather that legalistically and dutifully acting out some prescribed behavior.

Go After It

Since God is the Great Physician, our Healer, it makes sense to have a great relationship with him. If we communicate together in prayer, we can work together. If we listen to him in his word, we will know what he is thinking. Once we know what he is thinking, we must then respond to that knowledge. "Our righteousness before God is simply based on fulfilling the demands of the relationship that he desires to have with us," says Fred Faller. God's righteous faithfulness in relationships should go unquestioned. Perhaps that is where we need to begin hungering and thirsting. Passages that express the righteousness of God are numerous. Consider the following: his righteousness toward us in Psalms 65 and 103; his righteous kingdom in Isaiah 32:1-8; his righteous purpose in 1 John 4: 9-11 and his righteous promises fulfilled on the cross in 2 Corinthians 5:18-19 and Ephesians 2:17-18.

To hunger and thirst for something implies a motivated search. I remember the intense hunger that motivated Michael's search for food at 5:00 a.m. while he was on Prednisone. Every morning he woke up famished. If I did not make it to the kitchen soon enough, I would find him sitting by the refrigerator crying. I was motivated to teach this six-year-old how to fix his own breakfast. Some mornings he would cook and eat five eggs and five pieces of toast.

Just as God gave us the drives of hunger and thirst to keep us alive physically, he has given us a hunger and thirst for him to survive and thrive spiritually. Hungering and thirsting for a right relationship with God can be compared to our going after our relationship with the person we want to marry. When I was engaged and even first married, I hated conflict in our relationship. I would do anything to resolve any threat to our "haven of bliss." As the years passed, however, I found that my desire for righteousness in the relationship gave way to the desire to be *right*. It became very important to me to prove who was right in each situation. Then I slipped into being self-righteous about our relationship—I was certain that I was *always* right.

Unfortunately, after years of unrighteous conflict, I found myself totally complacent about our marriage relationship. I did not care anymore. God had to shake us up at the very core of our decaying relationship to get us to see the destructive patterns that we had allowed to develop. In the same way, God can see the deterioration of our relationship with him whether we can see it or not. He will try with all his might to wake us up to see it too. God hates unrighteous conflict, but he hates self-righteousness and complacency even more. It makes him want to vomit (Revelation 3:16). After rebuking the complacent women of Jerusalem who had self-righteously nibbled at religiosity to the point of spoiling their spiritual appetites, God says, "The fruit of righteousness will be peace; the effect of righteousness will be quietness and confidence forever" (Isaiah 32:17).

Look at your relationship with God. Do you still desire it above everything else, or do you think you are religious enough for God? Have you gotten totally complacent?

For most of us, our lives are filled with so many comforts and activities that rarely do we sit still and feel our hunger pangs for righteousness. Hunger pangs can be ignored to the point of starvation. Neglected babies, left to die, eventually stop crying for food. Silent hunger goes unfed. Can critical illness and pain become a blessing? Yes, because our bodies are heightened to a sense of danger and our souls are stirred out of their slumber. When we face death and judgment or a life of suffering, the monotony of our daily lives is broken, and we are jolted into an awareness of eternal matters. Many questions rush to our minds: *How can a righteous God allow children to suffer? How have I offended you, God?* The consistency of clawing pain or disability peels away our phoniness and exposes our true character and faith. Our desire, or lack of desire, to respond righteously to God will determine the outcome of our spiritual, emotional and physical health.

What has dulled our appetite for spiritual growth and physical and emotional well-being? Have we let busy schedules, frequent failures, discouragement, boredom, selfishness, bitterness or a weak will dull our appetites? Many "experts," such as physical fitness guru Richard Simmons, say that the motivational key to fitness is to love yourself. "Yeah, sure, Richard, but what if your self-esteem is so low that you have to look up to see the cracks in the floor?" As I have already mentioned, I have personally struggled much of my life with clinical depression as a result of a genetic problem, hormonal imbalances, radical cancer surgery and medication. In short, I just naturally lacked many self-motivating "juices." People who are more naturally motivated often cannot relate to this. So where and how do we get that vital motivation to live well and righteously? I have tried tying myself onto a motivated person's bumper and being dragged along behind, but that's not much fun—and it has proven dangerous! We must each get from God our own motivation to be righteous.

A hunger and thirst for life itself has motivated me to get vital health care for my children and for myself. To turn our doctors' attention to finding the cancerous cause behind Michael's and my own health problems took some indignation, proving the old adage that persistent patients get the cures. When you are dealing with life-threatening issues you cannot afford to be complacent.

Motivation Is the Key

Motivation is the key to growth and development in any area of life. For many years I worked with deaf children and children with other special needs. Getting a child to try to speak or walk when it is uncomfortable, painful or a seemingly useless effort, takes work. One little guy who has touched my heart eternally is David Simeone. David was born with spina bifida, a congenital defect in the walls of the spinal canal allowing the spinal cord to protrude, which results in paralysis to the body below the point of exposure. He was not able to walk unassisted. When David was about two years old, he also suffered a shunt blockage that caused some damage to the speech center of his brain. Although he had been able to speak before, he lost this ability. My role as his one-on-one assistant

was to motivate him and support the speech and physical therapists' efforts.

During my two-and-a-half years of helping him in all types
of situations, I learned much about what motivated him. I also
saw the incredible effort of the team of teachers and therapists
to help him make gains. As his teachers, we could see the ben-
efit of his learning to talk again and walk with crutches, but to
David, some days it was just not worth the pain and the effort.
It was embarrassing for him to babble instead of talk like the
other four-year-olds. The atmosphere in the classroom was incredibly stimulating and inspiring, but David was the one who
had to *choose* to walk and talk. By the end of the school term
and just before our move to Los Angeles, David finally spoke.
After successfully putting a simple puzzle together, we heard
him exclaim, "I did it! I did it!" To the cheers of the entire
preschool, he even walked in his walker without assistance.

The emotion and joy that I felt at that moment can barely
be expressed. It was better than watching my own children
take their first steps and babble their first *da-da*s. It was more
like the joy that I felt when the doctor said, "Mrs. Lamb, there
are no more signs of cancer in your son." I knew that these
first steps would be the most important ones in David's life. I
did not realize that they were about to become some of the
most important steps in my life, too.

I thought I had already learned a lot from God during
Michael's cancer and my cancer experiences, but God used my
teaching experience with David Simeone to show me that I
still needed to learn more. I was like David in that there were
areas in my life in which I was still unmotivated and handicapped, spiritually. I was also resistant to change in areas that
were hard, painful, embarrassing or ones in which I had experienced frequent failure. Even though surrounded by the best
support team, I was afraid to push myself emotionally and
physically in situations that exposed my weaknesses. Loss of
memory, depression, body pain, extreme fatigue and weight
gain plagued me the most. (One medication that I take is also
prescribed to underweight people who specifically *need* to gain
weight!)

I had lost my appetite for righteousness again. I was only nibbling at it. God was showing me that I needed to stop pridefully resisting help, deny my self-protection and take some steps in faith. I can still feel the pain and humiliations flare up at times, but now I think of David Simeone, my support team and most of all, the cross. Remembering the pain and humiliation that Jesus endured for my soul's healing deeply motivates me to push past any personal pain and humiliation. It motivates me to go after my relationship with God, no matter the cost.

Motivated by God's Love

For I am convinced that neither death nor life, neither angels nor demons, neither the present nor the future, nor any powers, neither height nor depth, nor anything else in all creation, will be able to separate us from the love of God that is in Christ Jesus our Lord.

Romans 8:38-39

God has a much stronger motivation for me to be righteous than I have; therefore, I borrow God's motivation frequently. When I think about why he has blessed me with life, healing, love and salvation, in spite of my sin and ingratitude, I honestly cannot comprehend it. But *his* motivation is clear—he loves me, values me and believes in me. He sees me as his child in need of love, protection, guidance and discipline. He knows me well enough to know how to personally motivate me. I need to accept his love and be intensely motivated to respond righteously out of gratitude to him.

Motivated by God's Joy

Consider it pure joy, my brothers, whenever you face trials of many kinds, because you know that the testing of your faith develops perseverance. Perseverance must finish its work so that you may be mature and complete, not lacking anything.

James 1:2-5

Creative approaches to teaching are not a foreign concept in Janet Hammonds' aforementioned preschool classroom— one in which special needs children are included with other children. One Halloween I went to work there dressed as a clown. Amazed at the enthusiasm of the children to try new skills for me as a clown, I contemplated permanently giving up my cardigan sweaters. What was work yesterday was suddenly fun and exciting for them.

Similarly, God arouses our curiosity by telling us that something will be a joy, even if it does not *feel* like a joy right then. Rejoicing while suffering does not immediately make sense to us, but not wanting to miss out on any fun can motivate us to find the joy in our tragedies. God shows us that joy is found in the process of growing and maturing through our difficulties.

Motivated by God's Warning Signs

Borrowing the faith and enthusiasm of teachers, classmates, friends and family can give us the boost that we need to get over the humps, but sometimes it takes more than a boost. Suffering itself can be enough to motivate us to learn new skills and develop new health habits. God always warns us in his word of things that will harm us. Just as the pamphlets in every medical clinic tell us the "Warning Signs of Cancer," so God lists the spiritual warning signs of unrighteousness in Galatians 5:19-21: "hatred, discord, jealousy, fits of rage, selfish ambition and drunkenness" and others. Choose to ignore the warning signs and die, or be motivated by them to change and live.

We human beings ignore warning signs all the time. Chris Chloupek, a young ministry leader from L.A. expresses it best with his Brooklyn accent: "Every day you see people carrying around packages of cigarettes that say, 'Warning! The Surgeon General says if you smoke dese tings you gonna die!' Then you see the guy pull out one and light it up and say, 'How ya doin'?'" So true! We do not heed the warnings because we do not think they apply to us or somehow it is impossible for us "in our situation" to obey.

God never asks us to do the impossible, but he does challenge the areas that we think are impossible. Being righteous
in the midst of suffering seemed impossible to Roger and me
until God showed us how. But, it took a highly motivated
search. The warning from Jesus that we could gain the whole
world yet lose our souls was personally motivational (Mark
8:36). Why waste suffering on earth unrighteously and risk
suffering for eternity on top of it when the suffering here could
be all we would ever have to endure? The worst suffering to
waste, though, is Jesus' suffering. His suffering offers us life.
As is always the case on the road to maturity, we will not reach
our goal overnight. God works with us and helps us through
the faith-building process.

Righteous in Every Situation?

During Michael's battle with leukemia, the Star Wars movies were popular. For us, they became a full-blown, theater-
sized visual reminder to stay righteous in attitude as well as in
actions. In one dynamic scene, the evil Emperor destroys the
Star Wars fleet right before Luke Skywalker's eyes. Luke's pain
and anger are intense as he grieves the unjust loss of the lives
of his friends. The Emperor hisses through his shiny green
teeth, "Feel your pain, feed your anger, kill Darth Vader." Luke
tries to resist the Emperor's taunts, but the temptation seems
more than he can bear. A fight to the death between Vader and
Luke ensues. Luke writhes in pain with each blow from Vader's
light saber.

Finally, Vader severs Luke's hand, enraging him even more.
Valiantly, Luke fights on and begins to overpower Vader. His
opportunity to kill him finally arrives, and with his light saber at Vader's throat, he hears the evil Emperor's enticing words
telling him to go with his dark side. At that moment, Luke
realizes that he is about to truly lose himself to the dark side,
and he lays down his saber. Every human emotion presses him
to scream "Unfair!" and "Kill Vader," but his righteousness
and faith in the good side of "the Force" keeps him from sur-

rendering to those voices from the darkness.

Seeing Michael constantly wearing Luke Skywalker underoos kept our own spiritual battle to stay righteous in the forefront of our minds. Satan was continually whispering in our ears, "Feel your pain, feed your anger, blame God." Like Luke, we were tempted to scream "Unfair!" and lash out. But God did expect us to be righteous in this difficult situation, and we found that if we were motivated to be righteous, God—the true "Force"—was there to help us.

Teach Me to Be Righteous

Suffering can be our best teacher. Hebrews tells us that Jesus chose to suffer so he could help us when we suffer. In Aramaic, which Jesus spoke, "to sympathize" meant "to suffer with."

> For we do not have a high priest who is unable to sympa-thize with our weaknesses, but we have one who has been tempted in every way, just as we are—yet was without sin.
>
> *Hebrews 4:15*

> During the days of Jesus' life on earth, he offered up prayers and petitions with loud cries and tears to the one who could save him from death, and he was heard because of his reverent submission. Although he was a son, he learned obedience from what he suffered and, once made per-fect, he became the source of eternal salvation for all who obey him.
>
> *Hebrews 5:7-9*

If Jesus had never experienced suffering till he reached the cross, would he have been prepared for it? I don't think so. If we are ever tempted to think that Jesus did not suffer as much as we do, we need to read Isaiah 52:13-53:12. He *chose* to suffer in order to save and heal us. Although Jesus suffered much more than just physically on the cross, we need a deeper appreciation of the physical pain he endured. The fact that he suffered without having even one unrighteous thought needs to motivate us to resist the temptation to be unrighteous in the midst of pain.

Similarly, the apostle Paul lived a hard life. His attitude toward hardship is seen in Philippians 3:10:

> I want to know Christ and the power of his resurrection and the fellowship of sharing in his sufferings, becoming like him in his death, and so, somehow, to attain to the resurrection from the dead.

If we, like Paul, are humbled instead of threatened by Christ's righteous suffering, we will say, "How did he do it? How can I respond as he did?" Our gratitude for his suffering will motivate us to want to be like him and righteously endure our own suffering.

Fill Me with Your Righteousness

The words "You will be filled" must be the most precious words that can be spoken to people dying of starvation and thirst. God's promise is to fill us, not just to offer us a few crumbs of his righteousness. He is the bread of life that will quell our hunger and the living water that will forever quench our thirst (John 6:35; 4:10). It is important that his righteousness fill us, and not our own.

We are not righteous simply *because* we suffer, but by *how* we suffer. Otherwise, we'd all invest in a bed of nails! We cannot be proud of our own righteousness because we don't have any (Romans 3:23). Righteousness on our own power is just filthy rags needing to be cleansed by the blood of Christ (Ephesians 1:7). We are *made* righteous. Jesus was made to be sin, so that we can be made the righteousness of God.

After God washes us clean, he fills us with his Spirit (Acts 2:36-38; Galatians 5:22-25). It is much better to be filled with his righteousness than consumed with (and by) our own self-righteousness. Being preoccupied with our physical condition and wearing our suffering like a medal for all to see will consume us, not fill us.

The temptation to be unrighteous while suffering is extremely strong. We end up giving in at times. At those points, the most righteous thing to say is, "I was wrong. Will you please forgive me?" The battle to respond in a right or wrong manner is especially heated when it comes to our children's suffering. (I can only guess how God must have felt to see his son so unjustly treated.)

One day Michael and I were waiting in the children's clinic with other children also bald from chemotherapy, pretending to enjoy the short diversion of peaceful playing, trying not to think about the upcoming dreaded procedures. The quiet calm of the room was shattered by the out-of-control screeching of a woman's voice. "I told you to stop crying!" she screamed. The next sounds we heard were obvious slaps and painful cries of a child. (She certainly was not administering controlled, biblical discipline.) The eyes of all the mothers and children widened as this demonic screaming came closer. The banshee entered the quiet of our little sanctuary, and tension filled the air. She did not realize that she had entered the den of protective lionesses. Eyes glared and nostrils flared as our frightened children crawled up into our laps. Inside my mind I could hear myself leading the pack with thoughts of *How dare she beat her sick child in front of our children! Isn't there enough suffering?! I've got a rope; let's lynch her!*

Fortunately, God had been working on my heart of compassion. Knowing that my own unrighteousness many times comes out of fear and frustration, I prayed to God to help me overcome my indignation and speak softly to the woman. "Are you having a problem? May I help?" I said. As I glanced over my shoulder, the lionesses were about to pounce on *me* now.

Hysterically, the young mother cried, "I don't know what to do. My baby has been screaming and crying for three days. I haven't gotten any sleep, and I am at my wits' end."

Taking a few minutes with her, I helped her change her baby. Immediately, I knew why the baby's screams were so familiar. Her little skin was raw from an allergic reaction to something in her urine. One of my children had experienced the same thing. When I explained to her that a wet diaper must have felt like acid on her baby's skin, the mother cried, and apologized to her baby.

"You poor thing, I didn't know you were in so much pain. I am so sorry."

God's righteousness had another victory that day. I learned that I could trust him to help me overcome the unrighteousness in my own heart and life. As I have continued to hunger for his righteousness through the years, he has continued to fill me and bless me with an ever-deepening relationship with him. As I have sought to please him, the definition of true righteousness, he has drawn me closer and closer to his heart.

14

The Joy of Giving and Forgiving

"Blessed are the merciful,
for they will be shown mercy."

Matthew 5:7

Jesus was looking forward to his return visit to Nazareth. Ah, home! Homecomings can be wonderful, but a bit strained at times. Especially now, it was difficult to come home to relax because of the Pharisees. They always show up and spoil everyone's fun with some sort of religious argument and stuffy folderol. At the very least it would be good to see his mother again.

In Jesus' hometown, people had little faith, thanks to the Pharisees, with their long robes and pious looks. They were always stirring up enough dust and dirt to choke out anyone's faith.

"I knew it was you," said Mary. "I saw the dust cloud coming. You and all your friends, come on in. Sit down. I'll go see if I have some fresh bread and honey for you boys. Uh-oh, Jesus—just as I suspected, here come those stuffy Pharisees right behind you.

In the meantime, Josiah, a paralytic, and his brother, David, were trying to convince three of their friends to take advantage of Jesus' visit home. "Please, he is my only hope. I'm sure of it," pleaded Josiah.

"Come on you guys" said David. "You know what a nuisance Josiah has become since he heard about Jesus' miracles. It will only get worse. We'll never have any peace until we at least try to get Jesus to see him."

One of the friends said, "I did see the man that they claim was healed of leprosy. His skin was like a newborn's.

"Come on you lazy mules, pick me up. Why, if I had legs that worked, I would..."

As they approached the house, the men and their paralytic friend were amazed at the crowd. "See what you turtles have done now? We'll never make it up to Jesus."

"Hush brother, I have a plan," said David.

Since they could not get him to Jesus because of the crowd, they made an opening in the roof above Jesus and, after digging through it, they lowered the mat the paralyzed man was lying on. When Jesus saw their faith, he said to the paralytic, "Son, your sins are forgiven."

Now some of the teachers of the law were sitting there, thinking to themselves, "Why, does this fellow talk like that? He's blaspheming! Who can forgive sins but God alone?"

Immediately Jesus knew in his spirit that this was what they were thinking in their hearts, and he said to them, "Why are you thinking these things? Which is easier: to say to the paralytic, 'Your sins are forgiven,' or to say, 'Get up, take your mat and walk'? But that you may know that the Son of Man has authority on earth to forgive sins..." He said to the paralytic, "I tell you, get up, take your mat and go home." He got up, took his mat and walked out in full view of them all.

Mark 2:4-12

If you were "Josiah," which would you have preferred: to be healed or to be forgiven? Would you have preferred being able to walk or having your heart purified and cleansed? Your answer reveals what you value the most. Forgiveness and mercy heal the soul, and relationships, for eternity. A physical healing will last only a lifetime. A person's health or lack of health does not necessarily reveal the state of his or her spiritual health. Jesus can discern the state of the heart, and he was hardest on those who were only interested in keeping up the external appearance of righteousness. He wanted them to focus on their debilitated hearts that were void of love and faith. Today we live in a health- and beauty-conscious society. At times the worship of "body beautiful" seems to elevate its practitioners to near godlike status. Before I'm hauled away and chained to a StairMaster as punishment, please hear me: I do believe in being good to your body, but God puts our spiritual health as the higher priority (1 Timothy 4:8).

If we find ourselves thinking that God is unmerciful toward us because he has not healed us physically, we need to think again. This same God sent his son to die for us so we could be forgiven, so that we could have meaning and purpose in our lives. In his mercy, he paid the highest of prices so that we could be with him for eternity.

Through a Child's Eyes

Throughout my growing-up years, I received a glimpse of a merciful God. My father was hospitalized for nearly a year, and my mother was left alone to care for five little children. At one point, the pressure and poverty were so great that she considered putting my brother and me in foster care. I watched my mother's incredible faith emerge as she put our future in God's hands. We prayed daily for my dad's health to return.

Our family was looked down upon because my father was hospitalized for a nervous breakdown. (World War II and a flock of children had taken their emotional toll.) We were not considered "active" members of our church, so there was little help offered. But my mom looked pretty active to me as a six-year-old. Mom didn't drive, so on the days that she did get us rides to church, she would send us a few at a time. If we all went, we would go on Sunday night because it took so much time and energy to get all five of us ready. (Our ages ranged from six months to eight years.) God heard Mom's prayers, and Dad came home a stronger man. The seeds of faith in a merciful God were planted deep in my heart.

Where's the Mercy for Me?

As an adult, I had to learn to recognize God's mercy. It did not always look the way I thought it would or should. How many times have you been offered mercy that did not *feel* like mercy? We don't have a clue, do we? Because the spiritual battle for our souls is being waged on a level that we can't even comprehend, we have no idea how much mercy we are being given moment by moment. In the book of Job, Job probably had no knowledge of the discussions that God and Satan were having. All he knew was that he was suffering. He did not know that God would not allow Satan to carry out his full-blown plan to destroy Job. God promises that his plans for our lives are somehow for our good:

> "For I know the plans I have for you," declares the Lord, "plans to prosper you and not to harm you, plans to give you hope and a future. Then you will call upon me and come and pray to me, and I will listen to you. You will seek me and find me when you seek me with all your heart".
> *Jeremiah 29:11-13*

He plans to prosper us and give us hope. Do we believe that? Our faith is on the line because "without faith it is impossible to please God, because anyone who comes to him must *believe* that he exists and that *he rewards those who earnestly seek him*" (Hebrews 11:6, emphasis added).

Every challenge in the lives of his children has to first be "quality checked" by God to make sure that it is not more than we can bear (1 Corinthians 10:13). Through our faith in him, God shields us by his power (1 Peter 1:5). Keep in mind that a shield has no other function except to protect. Anything that God allows to penetrate his shield of protection must somehow be for his purposes. And when we are committed to his purposes, "we know that in all things God works for" our good (Romans 8:28).

This may sound weird, but we all actually need to be more merciful toward God, because we have no idea what he has had to go through for us!

I once heard a story about an angel who visited two farmers. The first farmer was cruel and greedy. He made the angel sleep in the barn and offered him no food. During his stay, the angel repaired the barn wall and watered the farmer's cattle.

The second farmer was a kind and generous man. He gave the angel food and a warm bed by the fire. However, the next morning the farmer woke to find his best cow dead and his well dried up.

On the surface it seems as if the angel were unfair to the good farmer and too kind to the greedy one. However, what the farmers could not know was that the angel found money hidden behind the barn wall of the first farmer. He sealed it up to keep the greedy man from finding it. The underground stream that filled both men's wells had become polluted. To protect the good farmer, the angel dried up his well. But what about the death of the good farmer's cow? The death angel had visited the good farmer's home that same night, but the angelic guest persuaded him to take the cow instead of the man's wife. So, until we get to heaven, we won't know all of the ways we have been protected from day to day. Let's look for the good, trusting that the God of mercy and goodness is orchestrating plans to prosper us.

Appreciating God's Forgiveness

The parable of the unmerciful servant in Matthew had always confused me. I could not understand why the servant who was forgiven of his debt of several million dollars could not forgive his friend the pitiful few dollars that he owed.

But then I saw that the man totally missed the whole wonderful, outrageous gift of forgiveness! Possibly he did not hear or did not comprehend that the master had just forgiven his million dollar debt. Perhaps all he could hear were his own thundering thoughts such as *I don't take charity. I've got to pay him back. How will I ever pay him back? I don't trust him. He'll pull up this debt again; I know he will.*

Until I accepted fully the forgiveness that God offered me through the gospel, I carried around a debt-filled mind-set. There is a point in each one of our lives when the debt is not just a *feeling*, but a *fact*. Before I became a disciple, I needed to see that my debt of sin was not just a feeling, but a fact. My relationship with God was not right. I needed to examine my life and the Bible to realize that I, personally, had never yet fulfilled the terms of the agreement for forgiveness by God. I had always approached him on my terms, not his. (See Matthew 7:21-23.)

But even after God forgave me, I was always worried about what I owed God or what God owed me. It took my allowing God to forgive me for specific sins in my life before I was truly set free. I had to imagine taking Jesus into specific situations and watching him react to *me* as he had reacted to similar people in the Bible. For example, my guilt over impurity did not go away until I remembered how Jesus treated the woman caught in adultery. John 8:1-11 tells us that she was brought before him to be stoned, as the law allowed, but he did not stone her. He challenged the crowd to have mercy and they left. To the woman he said, "Then neither do I condemn you. Go now and leave your life of sin." Not condemned by God? I finally heard it and believed it!

Along with not hearing God tell us that he has forgiven us, we often do not hear the bottom line of how *much* he has forgiven. The servant may have understood perfectly well his master's forgiveness, but he may have been totally out of touch with the incredible amount he owed. In a word, we can be very self-centered and self-righteous. The little bit that others have done to us looks colossal in our eyes compared to what we think we have done to God. We often do not total up the debt that we owe God. The first step of extending forgiveness is remembering how gigantic our debt to God is.

We need to make sure we don't underestimate the power of God's mercy. James shows us how forgiven sin and healing of the body go together:

> Is any one of you in trouble? He should pray. Is anyone happy? Let him sing songs of praise. Is any one of you sick? He should call the elders of the church to pray over him and anoint him with oil in the name of the Lord. And the prayer offered in faith will make the sick person well; the Lord will raise him up. If he has sinned, he will be forgiven. Therefore confess your sins to each other and pray for each other so that you may be healed. The prayer of a righteous man is powerful and effective.
>
> *James 5:13-16*

God does the forgiving; confessing our sin in some way activates the healing. Hidden sin affects our bodies with stress, anxiety and other maladies. Although illness is not necessarily a result of sin in our lives, sin that is not confessed and not dealt with can accelerate and exacerbate physical conditions. Accepting God's mercy frees our minds and bodies to fight disease and restores stolen energy. Healthy acceptance of mercy also enables us to extend mercy to others, which frees us from bitterness, another sin that robs us of disease-fighting energy.

Forgiving Ourselves (Our Bodies)

You let me down again.
Betrayed by a trusted old friend.
You are "as reliable as a faulty bow" (Psalm 78:57).
The pain, oh yes, the relentless pain you have caused me. If it were not for this, my life could be so much different, so much better.
The ugliness and humiliation you bring me is almost unbearable. I feel like a tortured prisoner. I hate it. You have made my life miserable and lonely. No one wants to be my friend because of you.

Are these the thoughts of a twisted person who has been damaged by a close relationship? Actually, no. They are the thoughts that plague the minds of those who are unmerciful toward their own bodies. They reason, "My body should be a trusted friend. Why is it working against me?"

I had these types of negative feelings toward my body for many years. I felt angry at my sluggish mind, disgusted with my continual fatigue, irritated with the frequent pain in my arms and legs, frustrated with the malfunctioning of my female parts and impatient when I saw no immediate progress or improvement. I was very unmerciful toward myself. If my husband or close friends were to be as unmerciful toward me, I would certainly hope that they would repent. For some reason it is harder to extend mercy to oneself than to others.

Just as unforgiveness can hurt a relationship, I believe that my unforgiving and unmerciful attitude toward my physical body impeded my healing. Just as God's spiritual body (the church) cannot function properly without merciful attitudes within (1 Corinthians 12), so my physical body needed an atmosphere of mercy in which to heal. How do you suppose God felt about my criticalness toward my body? How do you think he responded toward my ingratitude for this "earthly tent" he had given me for a dwelling? (2 Corinthians 5:1-10). Being merciful and helpful to our imperfect bodies is an important step in healing. Forgive your body. You might even need it to forgive you too!

Compassion and Mercy Toward Others

Erica Kim is the wife of Frank Kim and mother of two precious girls, Miyoko and Manami. The Kims are people who have let God determine their path and use their many talents to spread the gospel. Erica's courage and effectiveness, despite having lupus, is an inspiration to disciples all over the globe. (She tells more of her story in Chapter 21.)

Erica and Frank became disciples while attending college in Boston, Massachusetts. Their dreams to serve God have taken them into teen ministry, on a mission planting to Paris, France, and finally to Tokyo, Japan, in May, 1989. Through faith and determination to persevere under restrictive health issues, Erica has experienced full recovery. The church in Tokyo has grown from 95 disciples in 1989 to 436 by the end of 1995. During her ordeal with lupus, Erica learned much about being merciful toward others. She says that before her experiences with physical challenges, she simply felt sorry for those who were dealing with physical problems. Now she has deep empathy and compassion.

In much the same way as Erica, our Michael has become a more compassionate person as a result of his leukemia experience. Besides his obvious love for children, he has developed a sensitivity to the underprivileged. Both he and his brother David were part of the HOPE Youth Corps during the summers of 1994 and 1995. This group of dedicated teens have gone into projects that HOPE Worldwide serves and sponsors. In 1994 they went into the poverty-stricken "Smokey Mountain" of Manila, Philippines. They helped families by bringing clothes and medical supplies to those who have built their homes on the garbage heaps of Manila. In the summer of 1995, they served in the HOPE work to AIDS patients in Soweto, South Africa. Our whole family has become more sensitive to the needs of the poor and underprivileged. Because we have been treated so mercifully, we have also taken seriously the privilege of mercifully meeting other people's spiritual and physical needs.

A Parent's Greatest Reward

As a parent, seeing your children become merciful to each other is perhaps the greatest reward. I am certain that God especially feels that way when we are merciful to each other in his family, the church. The Bible is full of references to the necessity of giving mercy to receive it. Seeing your child extend mercy at the risk of his own life is perhaps one of the most terrorizing and rewarding experiences a parent can have. I am grateful that I did not have to see what Mary, Jesus' mother, saw when he was on the cross. However, if we raise our children to make Jesus their Lord, they will have their own crosses to bear.

I remember a time when my eyes were fixed on Michael as he told me what had happened to him at church camp. I felt a pit in my stomach when he said, "Mom, I almost died." A rush of memories of hospitals and emergency rooms splashed through my head, and my heart began to pound. Then he shared the dramatic details of the near-drowning accident of a tall high school boy nicknamed "Tree." Michael was in junior high then. I could hardly breathe as he told me about the panic that he felt when he tried twice to rescue him. Instinctively, the boy was kicking and pulling Michael under with him. Finally, Michael punched him in the stomach to get him to let go and then swam down behind him and shoved him over and over until he reached an outstretched hand. Lord, have mercy...and he did—again! Though frightened, I was proud of Michael's commitment to show mercy to a drowning friend.

Extending mercy is a risk at times, but God has taken the ultimate risk by extending it to us. And he expects us to extend it to others.

It is God's deep desire to set up a cycle of mercy in our lives. He daily shows mercy to us. As we pass that mercy along to others, we are emotionally and spiritually healthy; our physical health also benefits even if we are not totally healed of our infirmities. But the parable of the unmerciful servant makes it clear that if we do not show mercy to others, ultimately God will not show mercy to us. Seek to know and see clearly God's mercy in your life, so God can continue to bless you as he desires.

15

The Wellspring of Life

"Blessed are the pure in heart,
for they will see God."

Matthew 5: 8

What if I said to you, "Here, have a glass of lemonade. It's not totally pure; it does have a few drops of sewage in it. That won't bother you, will it?"

How would you respond? I'm sure you would not be feeling too great about our relationship or my reliability. None of my excuses would be acceptable, no matter how sincerely spoken. The only lemonade you would be interested in drinking is 100% pure lemonade.

We are very concerned about maintaining purity of the food we take into our bodies. But are we concerned about maintaining purity of heart? As I have indicated earlier, Jesus wants to give us a remedy for the soul, mind, body and spirit. We need to understand the value of purity of heart in our healing process. Obviously, the polluted lemonade in the illustration would prove extremely hazardous to our health, but we need to look on a deeper level at purity of heart and its relationship to our physical and spiritual health. Even more deadly is impurity of heart.

What does it mean to have a pure heart before God? Building on the concept of having a righteous relationship with God, it is important to have pure motives toward God and to believe that he has pure motives toward us. If having this type of pure heart is a prerequisite to seeing God, it is of utmost importance to find out how to have one. Several initial responses come to mind:

(1) believing God and his word
(2) living by faith and not second-guessing or distrusting
    God's motives
(3) not wanting a relationship with God or others for

selfish reasons, but thinking of the needs of the other
(4) being honest about what you are really thinking, not
just seeking to please others

The Scriptures warn us to keep a close watch on our hearts
and give us some clues as to how to do it:

> Above all else, guard your heart,
>   for it is the wellspring of life.
> Put away perversity from your mouth;
>   keep corrupt talk far from your lips.
> Let your eyes look straight ahead,
>   fix your gaze directly before you.
> Make level paths for your feet
>   and take only ways that are firm.
> Do not swerve to the right or the left;
>   keep your foot from evil.
>
> *Proverbs 4:23-27*

More than anything, from this passage we see that a pure
heart is something we must decide we want to have and something that we pursue.

To See God

One of the strongest motivations in my life to be pure in
heart is, of course, to be able to understand and see God as he
really is. Second, I want to help my children to see God. When
David was about seven years old, an incident happened that
powerfully affected my desire to keep a pure heart for the sake
of my children. David was mistreating a little friend by jerking
him around by the arm. Indignantly (especially because the
child's mom was there, too), I sent David to his room to await
his discipline. My lecture on how to treat people started as
soon as I walked into the door. David listened to me, then in-
nocently said, "But, Mom, you do that to me." Taken aback, I
stumbled with giving him the reasons why moms don't always do what is right.

With tears in his eyes, he said, "Please, Mom, always do what is right; otherwise, how am I going to know what is right?" Through the years, his words have rung in my ears.

I know myself well enough to know that the only way to produce right actions is by getting a pure heart. As Matthew 15 explains, everything spills out of our hearts: all of our love *and* our wickedness. If my heart is hardened (Hebrews 3:8), callous (Psalm 17:10), stubborn and rebellious (Jeremiah 5:23), bitter (Hebrews 12:15) or full of deceit (Proverbs 12:20), it is impure.

Our impure hearts not only handicap us, but they also handicap God. Our children's view of God, as well as their view of other people, will be influenced by our lives. Hypocrisy in any form gives God a "bad name." If we claim to be God's children, our hearts and lives should look like his:

God is light; in him there is no darkness at all. If we claim to have fellowship with him yet walk in the darkness, we lie and do not live by the truth.

1 John 1:5

Whoever claims to live in him must walk as Jesus did.
1 John 2:6

If we claim to be his disciples, people judge God by looking at our lives. Likewise, many of our own concepts of God may be wrong because of the wrong messages we picked up from those who taught us with their lives. Maybe you were served some "polluted lemonade" in your time!

By now you are probably thinking, *How is she going to connect physical healing with this discussion on pure hearts?* Good question. I sincerely believe that a major factor in letting God do his healing work stems from our heart. The Proverbs tell us, "A heart at peace gives life to the body" (14:30). Impure hearts of faithlessness, ingratitude and hypocrisy keep God's hands from performing lifesaving surgery. On the contrary, hearts that are full of faith, trust, gratitude and humility will free God to be able to heal. Peter writes, "His divine power has given us everything we need for life and godliness through our knowledge of him who called us by his own glory and goodness" (2 Peter 1:3). Just think, this verse says that his power gives us *everything* we need for *life* and godliness. I can think of a few life needs, can't you? When we are in the clutches of pain, debilitating disease and life-threatening illnesses, even just plain old life is a welcomed promise.

God's Plan for Purifying Hearts

How pure is your heart right now? Do you have pure faith and trust? If not, how do you get it? Remember that Peter says life (and godliness) needs will be met through our *knowledge* of God. The more we *know* about God, the easier it is to trust him to meet our needs. Notice that the verse did not say that our needs will be met by *feeling* close to God. Our feelings change day by day, but God's nature of love is constant. The more we know about God, the closer we will feel to him because he will draw us to him and to his perfect love.

God is love (1 John 4:16). To know God is to know what love is. Paul describes love in 1 Corinthians 13:4-8. As mentioned earlier, to define God's nature, we can insert "God" every time Paul uses "love":

> God is patient, God is kind. God does not envy, God is not proud. God is not rude, God is not self-seeking, God is not easily angered, God keeps no record of wrongs. God does not delight in evil but rejoices with the truth. God always protects, always trusts, always hopes, always perseveres. God never fails.

We need to let this sink into our hearts and minds. This is who loves each one of us. This is who wants to rule our hearts and purify them as his is pure. It may be a struggle to fully trust and believe these truths about God. That's not unusual at the beginning, so we must hang in there. But we need to challenge our disbelief. Why is it there? Who or what influenced us to miss seeing God's true nature?

We should accept these characteristics of God because they come from his true word, but remember we are in a spiritual battle and the enemy, Satan, is opposing our faith right now. To fight Satan, we need to get familiar with his weapons so we can be prepared for our counterattack. God's spies have revealed Satan's sneaky plan to keep our hearts hardened. We don't need a magic decoder ring to figure out the plan. Paul shows us how to thwart Satan's plan and to fight the battle for a pure heart.

> For though we live in the world, we do not wage war as the world does. The weapons we fight with are not the weapons of the world. On the contrary, they have divine power to demolish strongholds. We demolish arguments and every pretension that *sets itself up against the knowledge of God*, and we take captive every thought to make it obedient to Christ.
>
> *2 Corinthians 10:3-5, emphasis added*

Tearing Down the Barriers

As we noted earlier, there is a model in the preceding passage that applies very well to the internal battles in our own lives even though Paul originally wrote with another application in mind. Imagine that each of our hearts is the target (because it is). Both Satan and God want to capture it. God wants to capture it to fill it with his love and purify it. Satan doesn't have too many plans for our hearts. He just likes to collect these hardened trophies and display them on his shelf; and you better believe that he gloats every time he looks at them. As long as God doesn't have them, Satan is happy. He also fears that God's army of loving hearts may overtake his kingdom, leaving him with fewer trophies. Satan's most successful plan is to keep the knowledge of God away from us. Aware that the knowledge of God will meet all of our needs, give us fulfillment and win us to his side, Satan will pull every dirty trick in the book to keep that knowledge from getting into our hearts.

Walls Versus Vulnerability

God's plan is to demolish the barriers Satan tempts us to use, but we must call on God's help to tear them down. The first barrier Satan tempts us to set up against God are the "strongholds" (v. 4). Proverbs 21:22 says,

> A wise man attacks the city of the mighty
> and pulls down the stronghold in which they trust.

I like to think that our strongholds are the fortress walls that we erect around our hearts to protect us from being vulnerable. Out of fear of being hurt, we keep God's love out. We actually end up protecting ourselves from the very thing we most need. We keep God out by hiding behind our jobs, our families, our religious traditions, our self-pity, our superficial strength and even our "eggshell emotionalism." (Eggshell emotionalism is described as follows: "Warning! If you say or do anything to hurt me—or even make me *think* that you might hurt me—I will self-destruct, and it will be all your fault! So back off.") But if we surrender our strongholds we will see that his "perfect love drives out fear" (1 John 4:18).

Before we were hit with all our family illnesses, I was beginning to get in touch with my lack of faith. Much of it came as a result of my fear of the power of God. Having been to a church college, I had plenty of Bible knowledge, but my faith was pitifully small. I had become a good and reasonable "keeper of the law" and "fortifier of the wall of religiosity." My faith was so weak that I only prayed out of duty and never really had faith that God would answer. I first recall being challenged to "pray believing" while I was in college. Praise God, not everyone there was a Pharisee. I agreed to get together with some friends to pray on a weekly basis. I was so frightened when God started answering our prayers specifically, that I quit praying with them. I felt like I had gotten hold of something too powerful for me. It was just too spooky and unreasonable. Indeed, I had gotten in touch with something more powerful than I was: God Almighty, himself. It took a lot of work for God to help me overcome my fear of him and learn to employ the power of prayer. Prayer works. That scares Satan too; don't let him suck you into his panic.

During the time of Michael's illness, prayers constantly went up to God for his healing. I still meet people who tell me they prayed consistently for Michael, for years. In faith, I asked the elders of our church to pray for me and anoint me with oil before I had the radical surgery for cancer (James 5:13-18). Roger's mother suffered strokes that left her left side useless. Prayer helped her regain muscle and nerve function. Our daughter, Christie, underwent surgery for the third time for endometriosis and for other complications. Prayers for her healing went up from Los Angeles to Boston to Western Europe. I was again amazed by God when the doctor came to the waiting room to show me proof in laparoscopic pictures that there was absolutely no sign of endometriosis to be found in Christie's body. These are only a few times that we know God has answered our earnest prayers.

The first beatitudes, being poor in spirit, mourning and being meek, address the need to trustfully surrender to God. Our walls must come down to see that he loves us and will not reject us because of our weaknesses. Keep studying these beatitudes to the point of believing God's true nature. Let down the walls around your heart. There is true strength in vulnerability.

Arguments Versus Faith

Next comes hand-to-hand combat with "arguments" (v. 5). Arguing is second nature to too many of us. We mistakenly think we are being intellectual by arguing. What we do not realize is that arguing is a faith-killer. It becomes so habitual to argue that we forget how to stop. Our arguments can be outwardly expressed or hidden in our hearts as "doubts" and "hidden reservations." It is interesting how we can have more faith in our doubts than in God. When we are certain that the worst will happen, many times it does. Our negative faith also brings results...only on the negative side.

Satan prods us to argue with everything that God says or does. He knows that if we surrender to God in faith, God can quickly get to our hearts. All the arguments of "Yes, but," "I never did it that way before," "That doesn't make sense," "It's too hard," "It will never work for me," will keep us busy swinging our defenses against God. We are so busy swinging, that we do not see the protecting shield of faith that God is offering us. We don't realize that God only wants us to surrender so he can set us free. The sword of truth in his hand, the Bible, *will* set us free: "If you hold to my teaching, you are really my disciples. Then you will know the truth and the truth will set you free" (John 8:31-32). Satan knows that God's desire is to set us free from Satan's clutches, so he keeps us swinging those arguments: "How do I know if the Bible is inspired?" "God doesn't expect me to take it seriously, does he?" "But what about those natives in Africa?"

Satan also knows that if we let God's sword get close enough to cut us deeply (Hebrews 4:12), we will see our own exposed hearts of faithlessness. Our false belief system, our doubts and our arguments would be exposed, and we would begin to realize that we are fighting against the wrong one. Satan and the lies that he feeds us are the real enemies. The diagnosis is finally made clear. It is lack of faith in a totally trustworthy God.

Did you ever argue your diagnosis with your doctor? How did you feel when he showed you the blood test results, the X-rays, the CAT scan, the EKG results? The fight may last a while, but eventually, you have to believe the results to get to the cure. Knowing the results is better than not knowing. Even though the news might be painful, at least you know what you are fighting. You've seen people who, in spite of the evidence presented by their doctors, still argue to the point of death (literally). Are you arguing with God right now? How can he cure what you won't let him touch? Let his words touch your heart to comfort and heal you.

Pretension Versus Humility

The final component that Satan convinces us to use is "pretensions" (v. 5). These could be viewed as towers of arrogance and pride. From them we look down on God and feel superior to him. "I am above this foolish battle. I refuse to get involved and choose sides." We keep our hearts away from God's love by feeling that we are above needing him. We are self-sufficient. Besides, we want to stay aloof from the battle. Not get involved. Stay neutral. However, our neutrality and indecision becomes a decision for Satan. God says if we are not for him, we are against him.

We are sometimes too proud to admit our helplessness (poverty of spirit). We must humble ourselves and ask God's guidance. We must admit that we do not know what is best for us—either spiritually or physically. Then we must be discerning as we search for God's answers. Proverbs 16:21 says that "the wise in heart are called discerning."

Sometimes we act overly confident because we are afraid of death, pain, illness or helplessness. Our pride keeps us from admitting our fear, so we are blocked in our relationship with God and with other people.

For whatever reason that we hold ourselves aloof from God and try to "do it [our] own way," we are setting up a high wall of pretension.

When we seek guidance from God and others in the battle for our health and physical life, our thinking becomes clearer and more decisive. Some of us wallow around with questions such as "How shall I attack my illness?" "What is the best medical treatment?" "Should I just pray and not take medicine?" "Holistic medicine, Eastern or Western medicine—which is more spiritually correct?" My advice is, whatever you choose to do, pray for wisdom, look for answers and then follow the course of action wholeheartedly.

Some may ask, "Do I have less faith because I am taking medication?" To me, many modern medical treatments are God's answer to prayers of faith for help. I also agree with many holistic approaches that treat the whole person and build up the body's own line of defense. I believe they can work together. But what I believe is not as important as what *you* believe, because it is your faith and your body. God is serious when he says,

> If any of you lacks wisdom, he should ask God, who gives generously to all without finding fault, and it will be given to him. But when he asks, he must believe and not doubt, because he who doubts is like a wave of the sea, blown and tossed by the wind. That man should not think he will receive anything from the Lord; he is a double-minded man, unstable in all he does.
>
> *James 1:5-8*

To choose to do nothing about our fearful walls, faithless arguments and pretentious pride is to choose spiritual death and little promise of physical healing. The only way to victory is to let down our walls, stop the arguing and take a leap of faith out of the tower of pretension. Jump into God's arms. The only other way down from that lofty tower is to get pushed out, like prideful Jezebel. The landing is a bit messy (2 Kings 9:30-37).

Begin at the Thought Level

I, personally, need visual imagery. I am not even aware many times that I am opposing God until I "take every thought captive." For me and my "blender brain" (all my thoughts are whirring) that means literally capturing what I am thinking, writing it down and comparing it to God's word. Then I can ask myself if my thoughts are consistent with God's or if I am putting up walls, arguing or being pretentious. When I see my impure, faithless thoughts written out on paper and compared to Scripture, I can ask myself, "Are these just feelings I have, or are they the true facts?" (Example: "God doesn't love me anymore" is my *feeling*. Compare to God's true *fact* in Psalm 136:1-26: "His love endures forever," repeated 26 times for emphasis.) I learned to communicate my faith and feelings more accurately as a result. When people would ask me what I was feeling, I would answer, "I can tell you what I am feeling, but that will change soon, so I would rather tell you my convictions." (This dialogue is especially helpful for women to use with their spouses during monthly periods of "hormonal insanity.")

Getting real about our true feelings and beliefs will help us be healthier. So often we have shut off our feelings and shut off our pain to the point that we have lost touch with reality. If we strive to be truthful with God and ourselves, we will actually be more aware of what is going on in our bodies physically. We will be able to distinguish between sin, depression and plain old fatigue. We will be able to help the physicians working with us.

We cannot always see our own heart's condition clearly and accurately. That is when we must trust that God will use other people to help us to see. Jeremiah 17:9 says that "The heart is deceitful above all things and beyond cure. Who can understand it?" I am grateful for people in my life who know me well enough, and who know God well enough, to help me get my heart purified and keep it purified. I am especially grateful to God for my husband, Roger. He is a man of incredible faith and integrity. He loved me enough not to let me get away with faithlessness and doubts. He persistently chiseled away at any walls I tried to erect. He loved me so much that he was willing to take the risks of "spiritual battle" with me. I know if he had not been in my life, I would never have survived. His reminder—"God is still in heaven; Jesus is still at his right hand, and the Holy Spirit is still in you"—continues to boost my faith.

To see God's true nature and to see God working in our lives and health conditions, it takes having a pure heart. We know that the barriers to a pure heart are walls of distrust, defensive arguments and pretentious, double-minded pride. There are so many aspects of our health that we have no control over, but this we can control. We can have the faith that heals. We can pray the prayers that bring God's answers. We can believe.

We cannot purify our hearts by our own power, but when we have done all that we can do, we simply trust God with our hearts. That's when we are ready for lifesaving surgery—a heart transplant from the God who promises, "I will give you a new heart and put a new spirit in you; I will remove from you your heart of stone and give you a heart of flesh" (Ezekiel 36:26).

"Blessed are the pure in heart, for they will see God."

16

A Purpose, Even in Pain

"Blessed are the peacemakers,
for they will be called sons of God."
Matthew 5:9

Clutching cold hands that are touching death.
Blessed are the peacemakers.
Cleansing raw wounds where fingers once were.
Blessed are the peacemakers.
Holding little bodies burning with fever.
Blessed are the peacemakers.
Kissing faces scarred by fire.
Blessed are the peacemakers.
Searching streets where brave men dare not go.
Blessed are the peacemakers.
Giving an anchor to minds that are drifting away.
Blessed are the peacemakers.
Soothing scorching pain with a loving heart.
Blessed are the peacemakers.
Cheering the victories that go unseen.
Blessed are the peacemakers.
Healing the pains that go deeper than skin.
Blessed are the peacemakers.
Giving hope and a will to live again.
Blessed are the peacemakers.
Replacing fear with courage.
Blessed are the peacemakers.
Preparing the heart to say a final good-bye.
Blessed are the peacemakers.
Being nailed to a cross as an innocent man.
Blessed are the peacemakers

A Message for Survivors

We have been blessed by the tireless efforts of peacemakers and the greatest peacemaker, Jesus, more than we even know.

During Michael's bout with leukemia, we encountered different reactions from people. Some were eager to help us with whatever they could. They brought us meals, took care of our other children, offered transportation and sent cards and flowers to encourage us. Interestingly, these were not always people who had suffered great losses themselves. They simply saw our need and wanted to help. Another group of people avoided us completely. It was as if we were cursed, and they feared contracting the curse. I was most surprised by the reactions of people who had suffered similar tragedies. They would either totally avoid any contact with us, or they would be our comrades in the battle—nothing in between.

As mentioned earlier, our next-door neighbors had just recently suffered the death of their own child to leukemia. At first, they tried to help, but the pain was too great. I totally understood. Their sorrow was too fresh. They felt as if they were reliving Shane's agony through Michael. They were great neighbors. We spent fun time together and helped each other with baby-sitting, yard work and other neighborly things, but it took many years before we could feel comfortable talking on a deeper level.

A few others whose children had experienced cancer became our comrades in the battle, praise God! The greatest warrior was Michael's first-grade teacher, Mrs. Darding, whose son had just completed his chemotherapy. She was always there if we needed to talk—or needed other help. After our very first visit to St. Louis Children's Hospital, a four-hour drive away, I realized that I had left Michael's full month's supply of medication at the hospital. I was still in a daze. Mrs. Darding was there with the identical medication left from her son's treatment. She helped me know when to push Michael and when to let him rest. Seeing her fighting spirit, even after her own battle, inspired me.

After Michael was pronounced cured and was off his three-year protocol of chemotherapy, I went through a period of feeling helpless and depressed. The immediate battle was over and now I had to entrust him totally to God's hands. Each little fever or bruise on Michael set up a panic in me that had to be confronted with prayers of faith and hope. Eventually, I weaned away from panic and slowly found myself also avoiding giving my heart to anyone or anything that had even a remote twinge of tragedy. The return visits for follow-up exams served as reminders to me to be grateful and to remember other people who were going through troubled times.

Not long afterwards, my cancer was diagnosed. As much as I wanted to avoid that tragedy, I could not. God knew me well enough to see that my love of comfort, my cowardice and my conflict-avoiding was so deeply ingrained that he needed me to learn a major lesson. I needed to change. I shared earlier that I was complaining to God that this whole thing did not feel like love to me. I battled God. I battled with my will to live. I battled low self-esteem and depression. I battled the rebellion of my body parts. I battled being misunderstood. I battled with giving love when the natural "want-to" was not there. I battled self-pity, anger, loneliness, pride, ingratitude and the like.

About the time that I was getting really battle-weary, I remember reading Psalm 144:1-2:

> Praise be to the Lord, my Rock,
>   who trains my hands for war, my fingers for battle.
> He is my loving God and my fortress,
>   my stronghold and my deliverer,
> my shield, in whom I take refuge,
>   who subdues peoples under me.

It all began to make sense: God was getting me to toughen up. He was preparing me for greater battles that he wanted me to win: spiritual battles in which God was waging peace.

Peace at a Price

If you are like me, you like the sound of the word "peace." But peace rarely comes without a fight. I heard a disturbing sermon given by Jeff Morrell of Los Angeles on Christmas day, 1995. He helped me see that while we are all soothed by songs like *Silent Night* and messages of *Peace on Earth, Good Will Toward Men,* the night of Jesus' birth was anything but peaceful. Revelation 12 gives a spiritual view of that night:

> The dragon stood in front of the woman who was about to give birth, so that he might devour her child the moment it was born. She gave birth to a son, a male child, who will rule all the nations with an iron scepter. And her child was snatched up to God and to his throne.
>
> And there was war in heaven. Michael and his angels fought against the dragon, and the dragon and his angels fought back. But he was not strong enough, and they lost their place in heaven. The great dragon was hurled down— that ancient serpent called the devil, or Satan, who leads the whole world astray. He was hurled to the earth, and his angels with him....
>
> When the dragon saw that he had been hurled to the earth, he pursued the woman who had given birth to the male child.... Then the dragon was enraged at the woman and went off to make war against the rest of her children— those who obey God's commandments and hold to the testimony of Jesus.
>
> *Revelation 12:4-5, 7-9, 13, 17; 13:1*

"All is calm, all is bright" doesn't quite fit what was really happening in the spiritual realm. For his remaining time on earth, Jesus' life was a battle to gain our peace with God. He suffered, he served, he got his hands dirty, he was tired, he was beaten, he was misunderstood, he rebuked sin, he turned over tables, he touched diseases and he was hammered away at by our sin. He did whatever it took to disturb our concept of peace, to show us how to have God's true peace, and he still does whatever it takes.

Peace Through Gratitude

Are we grateful for our health or for our spiritual peace with God? How does anyone know it? How will God know it?

Does our life show our gratitude? Luke 17:11-19 tells the story of ten men with leprosy who met Jesus. Jesus showed mercy to them by cleansing them and sending them on their way to receive purification rites from the priest. But only one man came back to thank Jesus.

Our gratitude will be seen in our actions. Have we gone back to thank Jesus or are we still holding a grudge?

"Oh, I'm grateful for my healing, but I did not like the way he went about it."

"Well, actually, I did all the work. I am the one who had to walk to the priests."

"The cure was too simple. He didn't appreciate how much I was suffering."

"I did not deserve this suffering in the first place."

"Oh, I'll get around to telling him thanks, sometime."

"I just want to forget any of this ever happened, and go on with my life."

In contrast to these examples, people who return to thank God go forward serving the needs of others. I realize that people can be benevolent with wrong motives, but those who care for others long-term are some of the most grateful people I have ever met. I want to dedicate this book to those peacemakers. My own list of personal peacemakers would take up another volume. I specifically want to thank and honor Bob and Pat Gempel of Philadelphia, Pennsylvania, and all the people who work with them in HOPE Worldwide. These self-less servants have set up clinics in leprosy colonies in India, built houses for lepers and their families, cared for AIDS patients and babies in Soweto, South Africa, given new hope to drug and alcohol addicts in Philadelphia, and provided immunizations for children around our nation. Most of all, they have resuscitated our hearts to compassionately love others.

Peacemakers in Death

Precious in the sight of the Lord
is the death of his saints.

Psalm 116:15

I sat alone watching the darkening sky engulf the air around me. It was a dark moment for me personally. Discouraged and frustrated, I was revisited by the haunting memories of my failures, my defeats, my sin, my weakness and my pain. I had not purposely planned to stop here, I just needed to stop somewhere to think. As I looked up from the dirt, I had to laugh at the irony of my surroundings. On my left was a stark, lonely graveyard and on my right was our sons' well-worn soccer field. There I sat in the middle of what represented life and death to me. I needed to make the choice of how to live out the remainder of my life. God had given me powerful examples of saints who had lived every moment well and then joined him in heaven. Their courageous faith-filled examples helped me to choose to finish the race victoriously. Thank you Jane, Paul, Ellen, Greg, George, little Mike and Shane. You are precious to God and to me.

The battle is God's. Jesus is the Savior, not me. I cannot fix everything, but he does appreciate my efforts. I cannot give people faith. I cannot be saved for them. But I must have my own growing faith. I must "watch [my] life and doctrine closely, so that [I] may save both [my]self and [my] hearers" (1 Timothy 4:16). I must open my mouth and share God's truth and God's love with others. I will have defeats. When I have defeats, I dare not quit, because ultimately, I, too, will face death. Therefore, while I am still alive, when I face a defeat, I will praise God and start again with step one...being poor in spirit, mourning, being meek, hungering for righteousness, being merciful, being pure in heart and going on being a peacemaker—for my sake, for God's sake and for the sake of others.

Peace Through Purpose

To find purpose in suffering gives true peace. To realize that God uses suffering to refine our faith and our character gives meaning to it. But God gives us a purpose greater than any level of "self-improvement." Imagine! God honors us by giving us the opportunity to live life with the same purpose that he gave to Jesus: to be his ambassadors.

His disciples will certainly do all they can to heal physical wounds, but they will also go about healing spiritual wounds that will be healed for eternity. We all know the frustration of watching helplessly as someone is suffering physically. God does not leave us helpless when it comes to helping someone spiritually. He gives us the tools we need, revealed to us in his word, but we must first accept his eternal purpose for our lives.

> For Christ's love compels us, because we are convinced that one died for all, and therefore all died. And he died for all that those who live should no longer live for themselves but for him who died for them and was raised again. So from now on we regard no one from a worldly point of view. Though we once regarded Christ in this way, we do so no longer. Therefore, if anyone is in Christ, he is a new creation.... All this is from God, who reconciled us to himself through Christ and gave us the ministry of reconciliation: that God was reconciling the world to himself in Christ, not counting men's sins against them. And he has committed to us the message of reconciliation. We are therefore Christ's ambassadors, as though God were making his appeal through us. We implore you on Christ's behalf: Be reconciled to God.
>
> *2 Corinthians 5:14-16, 18-20*

Our family has been truly blessed since we have taken on the role of peacemakers for eternity. Seeing beyond the battle of the body into the soul gives us a purpose to our lives and to our own sufferings. It has also taught us that winning souls doesn't come without putting up a fight against Satan. God puts us through his "boot camp" of physical battles to make us tenacious and courageous enough to stay in the spiritual fight. Each victory is worth the pain suffered.

Through the years one of our greatest joys has been John and Nancy Mannel's story. The first time I remember meeting Nancy, I was sitting in a little room at the back of our church auditorium. David was just a few months old and he was colicky.

Nancy and John had just started coming to church as a result of their own children's love for our children's program. (They were part of our bus ministry in which we brought children to services.) Nancy came back to offer me some help with my crying baby. She was a peacemaker for me that day. Knowing that I needed to reach out to her as a peacemaker for God, I called her later to have lunch together. She immediately accepted and said, "Okay, where do you want to go?" Since I was still new at being a peacemaker, I panicked and told her I would have to call her back. In spite of my fears, God used Roger and me to introduce the Mannels to the gospel.

As we started studying the Bible with John and Nancy, we found out that they had put their house up for sale and had begun divorce proceedings. But, shortly before we met, they had decided to give it one more try. I'll never forget one of our times studying together during the height of a blizzard. We watched the snow pile up to the top of their fence outside as God was melting their hearts inside.

John and Nancy became disciples, and eventually, he became an elder of the church in Charleston, Illinois. Wanting to get their family involved in and surrounded by a growing teen ministry, they eventually moved to La Grange, Illinois, where we were living at the time. We actually all lived in the same little house for a month. (We felt like we were crowded into Noah's ark as the basement flooded on several occasions!)

The Mannels were an incredible help to Roger and me when I developed cancer. Their greatest gift to us was being our peacemakers. I remember sitting in their living room with Chris and Marty Fuqua, talking through the storms that would brew up in Roger's and my relationship as we tried to adjust to the changes in our lives.

The Mannels were also our partners in peacemaking. Somehow, in that incredible year, the Chicago church grew to an attendance of 1500. During our time together, we helped other couples to become Christians. Now, many of those couples are having a worldwide impact as peacemakers for God. John and Frances Thorne became disciples in our first downtown Chicago Bible study. John is now the administrator for a number of rapidly growing churches in Russia. Dr. Henry Cramer also became a disciple and encouraged his wife Lanna to study with us. Now Henry and Lanna are going to plant a church of disciples in Jerusalem in June 1996. I get chills thinking about how God used us at such a physically weak time in our lives. Imagine the peace they bring to these entire countries!

Watching John and Nancy disciple their own children through their teenage storms gave us hope and courage to trust God through ours. Their oldest son, Jeff, and his wife, Laurie, are now in the full-time ministry. Kevin and his wife, Sue, are building a Christian home for their two little girls. Holly is letting her light shine in Los Angeles. God has used the Mannel family as peacemakers for eternity.

When we moved to Boston, God gave us the challenge to begin a "daytime ministry" for artists and musicians. I was still in a lot of pain and my mind was in a fog because of physical and emotional problems mentioned earlier. Yet this group grew from about twenty members to 120 in a year and a half. We led that ministry until I just could not physically handle it anymore. Yet, keeping our purpose in focus was what kept me encouraged, fulfilled and at peace. During that time we became best friends with David and Coleen Graham, constantly studying the Bible together with other couples. It ripped our hearts when the Grahams were called to be a part of the church-planting team to Los Angeles in 1989. Yet, God used them to build an Arts, Media, Sports Ministry in the L.A. Church of Christ that now has 1,000 people attending on Sundays. This group is only one part of the fast-growing Los Angeles church which currently has an attendance of around 10,000.

Then God gave me a little "rest in the west." We moved out to the western suburbs of Boston to have our children closer to the heart of the teen ministry. Roger took on his new role as editor of the international church publication, *UpsideDown Magazine*. He also continued to lead a large family group with the help of our good friend, Betty Morehead, who was leading the women. Even though my role had changed, I felt at peace about it. God surrounded me with incredible friendships. I was able to go back to being a learner and doing a lot of spiritual rebuilding and refining as I was physically healing.

The physically challenged ministry, led by Dr. Doug Webber and Bill Sullivan, who suffers from multiple sclerosis, gave me a reservoir to draw from as I was trying to make sense of my life outside the full-time ministry.

It was at this point that I was able to learn from some of the best grassroots peacemakers, Betty Morehead and Mary Wynne Burns, who led the most successful daytime women's ministry that I have ever seen; Barbara Gentry (now Barbara Manuputy), who led the single mom's ministry and passed the baton when she got married; and Sheila Jones, who ministered to the working moms and career women in a ministry called "Nine to Five and Spiritually Alive." Jeanie Shaw and Kay McKean, talented, dynamic women, led these other women. Their greatest gift, besides soul-winning, is identifying and encouraging women to use their talents for God. (You can blame them and Pat Gempel for turning me into a playwright and author.) The time I spent with these great women, and the love and respect that they showed me, helped me to gain a peace with who I was and also helped me to identify gifts with which I could glorify God.

We moved to Los Angeles in July of 1994 and are again working side by side with David and Coleen Graham in spiritual battle. Their spiritual growth has been an inspiration and source of strength to us again. God puts the right peacemakers in our lives at the right time when we keep his purpose in clear sight. Being a peacemaker is the most gratifying experience in life. Roger and I determined to use all that God had given us and taught us to serve God in any capacity we could. God has pulled so many things together for us here. God blessed me with a great doctor, Dr. Karen Chen, who has helped me get stronger physically. He has opened the floodgates of blessings to us by allowing us to work closely with leaders from all over the world through our work with KNN (Kingdom News Network) and the *L.A. Story*. God's plan for our lives has been so much greater than we could have ever imagined—and all because we decided to be peacemakers! How blessed it is to be called children of God.

17

Remember the Reward

"Blessed are those who are persecuted because of righteousness, for theirs is the kingdom of heaven.

"Blessed are you when people insult you, persecute you and falsely say all kinds of evil against you because of me. Rejoice and be glad, because great is your reward in heaven, for in the same way they persecuted the prophets who were before you."

Matthew 5:10-12

By this time in Jesus' Sermon on the Mount, I am sure some listeners were hoping that he would end it something like this: "When you have learned all these attitudes, people will like you. You will be respected and admired. You will succeed in life. You will be healed of all your physical afflictions!"

But, no! He had to end it with "You will probably be persecuted!"

Hey! I want my money back. I did not come to hear this! I don't need this in my life. I get enough rejection; I don't need any more. He's probably never been sick a day in his life. Who does he think he is telling me to get ready for persecution? Why, I have a good mind to...well, half a mind to...

Be honest, haven't you thought the same thing? Why does Jesus put things the way he does? Isn't there a plan for a "kinder, gentler" generation somewhere? Living the Christian life is tough enough—now I get to look forward to persecution? Jesus just shot down every "way to success" course I ever took, and now he adds this!

On the other hand, there may be just enough of the "yeast of the Pharisees" in our hearts to get a self-righteous "rise" out of us. Yes, even the hearts of the sick and disabled can have a touch of pride and arrogance. If you are physically challenged in some way, you may be tempted to think, *All right! I've got my ticket into the kingdom punched because I have been persecuted. Did I ever tell you about the time that the kids at school laughed at me for the way I looked? Then, there was the time that I didn't get hired for a job simply on the basis of my handicap. This town purposely discriminates against us with no access routes for the blind and handicapped! I had everything going for me before, and then my body gave out.* If that kind of suffering ensures our "ticket" to heaven, then let's go break some legs!

Please, before you send a "hit" man out to my house, hear me out. Paul says "In fact, everyone who wants to live a godly life in Christ Jesus will be persecuted" (2 Timothy 3:12). In John 15:20, 21, 25 Jesus tells us the same thing:

> "'No servant is greater than his master.' If they persecuted me, they will persecute you also.... They will treat you this way because of my name....This is to fulfill what is written in their Law: 'They hated me without reason.'"

When we *seriously follow Jesus as his disciples,* we will be persecuted. We will receive the same reaction he did. So, we have to ask ourselves if we will continue to follow him.

When I first read the Beatitudes, trying to keep in mind the spiritual-healing and the physical-healing aspects, I was really puzzled by this last blessing: "Blessed are those who are persecuted for righteousness." In each of the other beatitudes there was something we could strive for in our hearts and lives. Persecution is not something we strive for. It happens as a result of our being like Jesus. By responding to life's stormy challenges with the heart of humility, meekness, righteousness, mercy, purity and with a mission to be a peacemaker, we will become like Jesus. Then, we will experience what Jesus experienced: persecution.

Satan uses persecution to try to stop the kingdom of God. If Satan can get us to stop and "lick our wounds" or run away in fear, he can stop our spiritual growth and progress and the spread of God's good work through our lives. In other words, we need to take persecution as a compliment—we are posing a threat to Satan!

There will be pain, injustice, hatred, persecution and hardship. Jesus said not to be surprised when they come. He also set us an incredible example of how to handle these inevitable hurts. He did not run away from them; he ran to the Father. He did not retaliate; he reacted so righteously that it convicted hearts. Good hearts were drawn to him while bad hearts wanted him crucified.

What about our lives? When people look at us, do they feel any conviction within their hearts? Are we a threat to Satan? Again, if we are physically challenged, do they see us as that invalid, that woman with cancer, that guy in a wheelchair, that young person with a speech and hearing defect, that "sickly" person, that deformed person or that old guy? Our goal is to be so much like Jesus that people would say of us, "Wow, there is a woman of faith. There is a man of conviction. His life really challenges me; I have no real excuses. By the way, did you know, he has multiple sclerosis?"

Persecuted or Pushed Away?

To prepare for writing this chapter, I talked with many people who have personally experienced critical illness, trauma and disabilities. When I asked, "Have you ever been persecuted?" I was initially told horror stories of ways they had been treated unfairly based on their disability or illness. Later, many of them would say, "But I guess that is not *real* persecution, is it?" To be fair, very few of us have experienced the kind of persecution that Jesus and his early disciples experienced. We have heard of disciples in other parts of the world who have been beaten, imprisoned and tortured for their faith. But in America, the most we usually experience is bad press, insults, lies and rejection.

Yet, being pushed away, rejected, misunderstood and mistreated is very destructive to people who are already fighting battles within their own bodies and minds. Kindness and understanding is what they desperately need, but too often the disadvantaged are seen as a bother to the "healthy." Mark Mathis is a disciple in Boston and recipient of the Disabled Employee Award for the entire US Army in 1993. I asked his perspective on how the physically challenged are treated. He responded, "The hardest thing to deal with is being ignored. At group gatherings, I often get treated like furniture. People have actually set their coffee cups on my wheel chair and leaned on it as they talked with other people. Unless I initiate, a whole evening could go by without a single meaningful conversation."

"Let children stare and ask questions," said a speaker and author named Betsy Wilson. While she was speaking, I could not help but stare at her face disfigured by cancer and subsequent surgeries. She believed that much of the prejudice against people with handicaps and deformities is because people have unexpressed fears. Somehow they secretly and irrationally fear that if they are closely associated with people who have physical challenges, they themselves might also be stricken. Children who are allowed to ask, "What happened to you?" may also want to know, "Does it hurt you?" and "Will it happen to me too?" Most physically challenged people do not mind these questions. It is the silence that is hard to take. In spite of all the obvious challenges that our family has gone through, only very few people ever asked, "What was it like for you?" or "What did you learn from this?" In all sincerity, I can think of only four people who ever asked me what it was like to go through my cancer ordeal. Since I am more prolific as a writer than a talker, I don't think this was due to my talking about it so much.

I appreciate the heart of people like Linda Howard who spent the night following my surgery at my bedside. I told her, "Linda, you don't need to stay. The nurses will be in here a lot tonight." Linda's reply was "I need to be here for my sake. I need to understand what you are going through."

Please ask questions. Please show an interest in people. Remember there is a soul, a real person beneath that shell of a body. The first woman I ever became close friends with who had cancer was a woman named Virginia Mills. I took her to her cancer treatments when I was a young mother with only one baby and she was an older woman, but I asked her, "How are you doing, really?" I remember her reply well, "My body is shot;

I probably won't make it, but my soul is doing great." I am so glad I asked. She gave me a spiritual perspective on life that has been a solid foundation for me. What if I had not asked?

Persecuted or Persecuting?

We are called to imitate Jesus' heart and attitudes, to encourage others as he has encouraged us:

> If you have any encouragement from being united with Christ, if any comfort from his love, if any fellowship with the Spirit, if any tenderness and compassion, then make my joy complete by being like-minded, having the same love, being one in spirit and purpose. Do nothing out of selfish ambition or vain conceit, but in humility consider others better than yourselves. Each of you should look not only to your own interests, but also to the interests of others. Your attitude should be the same as that of Christ Jesus.
>
> *Philippians 2:1-5*

Which group of people does he include or exclude here? Obviously, he includes everyone and excludes no one—physically challenged or able-bodied (or temporarily able-bodied).

Fear of the unknown is one of the reasons people stay ignorant and prejudiced in their responses to those who have physical disabilities. Job's friends, Eliphaz, Bildad and Zophar, spent days trying to figure out what horrible sin Job must have done to incur God's wrath. The only friend of Job's whom God did not rebuke was the one who advised Job to listen to God. Elihu suggested that God was using suffering to mold and train Job. The other three were judging Job—not truly knowing how God was working. Unfortunately, many of these same misconceptions are still influencing the ideas and attitudes toward physically challenged people today.[1]

Would it help if we started a campaign to rid the world of injustice, prejudice and all bias and hatred toward the physically challenged? Perhaps, if we could change the world by trying to change everyone else. I am certain this cause would receive generous support; however, the true answer begins with changing *our own* hearts, not by waiting for others to change. If you are physically challenged, what kind of attitudes do you harbor in your heart for ways you have been treated unfairly? What is you attitude toward the "healthy"? If you are able-bodied, how much compassion do you have for those who are physically challenged in some way? How much do you try to understand what they go through? Do you treat them differently than you treat others?

We must stand firm together against persecution that comes from those who do not accept the message. But, as disciples, we must make sure we don't persecute each other in any way. Jealousy and envy are two sins of the heart that tempt the physically challenged almost daily. These sins were at the heart of the persecution of Jesus (Matthew 27:18). We could easily begin to "persecute" the able-bodied ones among us by being bitter toward them, by being difficult to lead and slow to encourage and support—all because we envy their good health. God warns us that the result of envy is self-destruction: "A heart at peace gives life to the body, but envy rots the bones" (Proverbs 14:30). We are tempted to envy the healthy, the cured, the contented, the financially secure and the capable.

Jealousy has been a part of my sinful nature that God exposed well before any of my family became ill. God took my jealous heart and turned it to his advantage. Before I became a disciple, I saw that the source of my jealousy was my husband's great relationships with people and with God. This alarmed me—especially jealousy of his relationship with God. Paul said in Romans 11:14 that he took the gospel to the Gentiles to make Israel envious, "in the hope that I may somehow arouse my own people and save some of them." My envy of his relationship with God aroused in me a desire to have one of my own. Instead of continuing to persecute him (believe me, I did some of that), I realized I needed to respect and imitate him. So, at the first sign of envy, let us take these two scriptures in Proverbs and Romans and call out to God.

It is important, from time to time, to check our hearts concerning persecution. Am I being persecuted for my righteousness or for my bitterness? We will reap what we sow. If people avoid you or respond curtly and negatively toward you or constantly dismiss your complaints as petty, check for a plank in your own eye. Are you a bitter, negative and complaining person? Do people avoid being with you because your spirit is a "downer"? Are you always self-focused or anxious? Do people feel drained or refreshed after spending time with you? Sometimes our words may be all we have to meet the needs of other people. Let's use them wisely!

But I need to be open with how I'm feeling, you may be thinking. Yes, it's important for us to be open, yet *how* we share our feelings is just as important. Read carefully Ephesians 4:29-32. Don't cause static in the communication lines with a hypercritical or a "doom and gloom" manner. Negativity can become a habit. After focusing on Ephesians 4, go back to the chapter on being pure in heart and do some more "heart-cleaning."

Dogged or Determined?

The truth is that people's attitudes toward us do have an effect on us. However, sometimes our view of what people think is exaggerated or imagined. That is, we can imagine we are being persecuted when we are not. When I was teaching deaf students, they wanted me to interpret *everything* that was said by *everyone* in the class because they thought people were talking about them. But often these feelings of insecurity are not rational and often neither are our reactions. How do we shield ourselves from reacting? Take a lesson from a "dog":

> A Canaanite woman from that vicinity came to him, crying out, "Lord, Son of David, have mercy on me! My daughter is suffering terribly from demon-possession."
>
> Jesus did not answer a word. So his disciples came to him and urged him, "Send her away, for she keeps crying out after us."

He answered, "I was sent only to the lost sheep of Israel."

The woman came and knelt before him. "Lord, help me!" she said.

He replied, "It is not right to take the children's bread and toss it to their dogs."

"Yes, Lord," she said, "but even the dogs eat the crumbs that fall from their masters' table."

Then Jesus answered, "Woman, you have great faith! Your request is granted." And her daughter was healed from that very hour.

Matthew 15:22-28

Why did Jesus talk this way to this poor woman? When Jesus referred to the Gentiles as dogs, he must have been speaking tongue-in-cheek in a way that caricatured the typical Jewish view. It just was not Jesus' style to make derogatory remarks about the Gentiles. Early in his ministry he showed his willingness to risk life and limb for his commitment to them (see Luke 4:16-30). But even if Jesus made this statement with an obvious irony in his voice, it was still a reminder to this woman of the way most Jews thought of her.

But the woman's response teaches us something important. How did she react when she was classified with the dogs? Did she get indignant and leave? Did she break down and cry because her feelings were hurt? No, she went back to Jesus and asked again.

Jesus was visibly moved and responded to her by commending her great faith. Her faith and focus were on Jesus, who he was and what he could do. She was not going to let some category people had put her in thwart her mission to help her daughter. Did she think she was an unworthy dog when she asked Jesus for such a blessing? Maybe she did. She did not deny it anyway. Did she see a twinkle in Jesus' eye and catch the irony in his tone? Don't sell her short. She may have realized quickly just how differently Jesus was viewing all this. But, in any case, she needed help and she knew that Jesus was the only one who could help her. She *knew* Jesus. She *knew* that the healing would be based on who he was, not on who she was. That is so much like the very salvation that he offers us. We can ask for mercy on the basis of who *he* is (Psalms 51).

The self-esteem of people dealing with physical, emotional, mental and spiritual weaknesses is usually pretty low. Self-image can be even more distorted than our bodies. Remember, we are not viewed by God the way we view ourselves or the way others view us. The day I finally let this truth sink into my heart, I thought, "I feel like a dog. Maybe I am a dog. But God is not. I am determined to keep going back to him based on the reality of who he is, not on who I am. Prayers are answered because of who *he* is. People are cured because of who *he* is. I trust his plans for me because of who *he* is. I can accept his gift of salvation because of who *he* is. I will give God the glory for who *he* is."

The Reward Is Belonging

Having worked in the special education field, I have had incredible opportunities to hear speakers share their own experiences dealing with others' reactions to their physical challenges. Norman Kunz, an author and educator born with cerebral palsy, is especially inspiring. At the beginning of his presentation, we all felt a bit awkward for him as he tripped and nearly fell a few times. Changing the transparencies on the overhead projector was cumbersome for him. It was a real effort for him to speak clearly, yet the words he spoke gave a clear message. He spoke about the need to belong. Since he was talking to educators, he addressed the necessity of developing an atmosphere in the school and classroom that gave each child a sense of "belonging." Many of his points were based on time-tested biblical principles. By the end of his presentation we were inspired and challenged to make a greater effort to instill in each child a sense of value, worth and belonging. We had become so engrossed in his message that we almost forgot about his disability.

The reality is that we are all human. We are created in the

image of God and are spiritual beings. We are all tainted with sin and need forgiveness. But, unfortunately, many people are made to feel as if they do not even belong to the human race. God knows our need to belong is as strong as our need to feel valued and worthy of being loved. Jesus concludes his sermon by saying, "Blessed are those who are persecuted because of righteousness, for theirs is the kingdom of heaven." The kingdom—what is that? Some exclusive club or ethereal existence?

It is beyond the scope of this book to delve deeply into this rich biblical concept, but suffice it to say that passages like Matthew 16:18-19 show us that the church is God's kingdom on earth and those like Matthew 8:11 show us that the ultimate fulfillment of the kingdom will be in heaven when great friends sit down in fellowship and celebration. When Jesus talks about the kingdom, he is talking about *belonging.*

Since as disciples, physically challenged or able-bodied, we will be persecuted for sharing our faith and standing firm in our convictions, we need the sense of belonging that encourages and builds us up. To truly feel like you belong, though, involves being loved in a way that allows correction. Physically challenged people need tough love, although we may not always act like it. We like knowing that we are not just being "tolerated" or tiptoed around. We need to be called spiritually higher from God's word (2 Timothy 3:16). We can only help one another by communicating honestly about our realistic expectations, and then work together to help each other mature in Christ.

The church is a living, breathing spiritual organism, not a dry stuffy organization.

In 1 Corinthians 12, Paul describes the church as a body. If there is anything a physically challenged person does understand, it is how the body is *supposed to* function. The value of each part is especially vivid to us. Being ill has shown me how very much I need other people in my life. Not just to serve my physical needs, but my spiritual needs. Just as a finger that is cut off and left alone will die, so would I die without these relationships. I would die without the servant hearts of my dear friends in the deaf ministry. I would die without the example of Simone Bishop, who although suffering with polio and scoliosis, is a mom of two disciples in our ministry and adopted mom to all the rest of us. I would die without the courage of a young man named Sean McKean who is short of stature because of a birth defect, but a giant in his love for God and the kingdom. I would die without all of you, and you would die without me. We belong together.

Revelation 21:2-4 gives us a preview of what is in store for us in his kingdom in heaven:

> I saw the Holy City, the new Jerusalem, coming down out of heaven from God, prepared as a bride beautifully dressed for her husband. And I heard a loud voice from the throne saying, "Now the dwelling of God is with men, and he will live with them. They will be his people, and God himself will be with them and be their God. He will wipe every tear from their eyes. There will be no more death or mourning or crying or pain for the old order of things has passed away.

There will be no pain, no limits, no wheelchairs. Our physical imperfections will be gone. Paul writes,

> If only for this life we have hope in Christ, we are to be pitied more than all men.... So will it be with the resurrection of the dead. The body that is sown is perishable, it is raised imperishable; it is sown in dishonor, it is raised in glory; it is sown in weakness, it is raised in power; it is sown a natural body, it is raised a spiritual body.

> *1 Corinthians 15:19,42-43*

The troubles and storms of persecution and hardships in this life will be like a mist compared to an eternity spent with God and his family. Whether persecuted for our faith or for anything else, we are truly blessed by a loving God. To him be the glory.

18

If You Are Willing

When he came down from the mountainside, large crowds followed him. A man with leprosy came and knelt before him and said, "Lord, if you are willing, you can make me clean."

Jesus reached out his hand and touched the man. "I am willing," he said. "Be clean!" Immediately he was cured of his leprosy.

Matthew 8:1-3

He looks long and hard at the one who is speaking. Then he glances toward heaven, wondering. His gaze returns to his own skin, white with leprosy. He thinks...

I have never heard a man of God teach like this Jesus. He speaks with authority in his voice, and his teachings make sense to me. I have heard other religious men, but I have yet to have one of them even grace me with their eyes when I've cried for mercy. To know that they even acknowledge that I am human would give my old bones some comfort. But this Jesus, he puzzles me. Even though I am still sitting in this same old wretched body, I feel somehow renewed inside. Could it be hope that I am feeling? That's a laugh. To feel hope again is as foreign as feeling my wife in my arms again. If I had arms!

There it is again! Wow! This feeling could keep me going for days! But the pain will eventually drown out my joy again. How cruel hope is when death and pain keep thrusting my soul into the darkness.

Darkness? What was it the teacher was saying about a light shining in darkness? It would give light to the whole house if it were not covered up. Oh God, as this man spoke I felt him lighting up the darkest corners of my life. Not just the blackness of my rotting skin, but the blackness of my rotting soul. His words hurt like the blinding desert sun when he spoke of not hating or wanting revenge. In my heart I have murdered even though my body could not lift a sword. I have committed adultery through my lust even though I could not even crawl into the tent of a woman.

Then when he said to love your enemies, I was ready to close my ears until he said, *"Be perfect, therefore, as your heavenly father is perfect"* (Matthew 5:48). Can a man be as perfect as God? God knows I cannot be perfect with this imperfect body that he gave me. Why, that's unfair! But, wait a minute, could it be that he was not talking about perfect actions so much as he was talking about a perfect heart. My heart and spirit are not bound by this body, they are crippled only by my lack of faith and love. I cannot blame my leprosy for the sores of bitterness on my heart.

It's all beginning to make sense. Oh, please, befuddled mind don't fail me now. What else did he say? Blessed are those who are poor in spirit and the merciful and the peacemakers. But how can I change the blackness of this old heart? I have been full of anger, self-pity and resentment for so long. How can I ever hope to change it?

My head is throbbing from the heat and too much thinking. I cannot let myself think too much, or I will go crazy worrying about what it all means and why I am sick and who will take care of me and...and.... Now there's another laugh. Here I am worrying about worrying, and I am worrying myself sick. Didn't he say not to worry because God knows my situation and cares about me? Right! He said to pray to God by asking, seeking and knocking. He said that God would hear me.

I can't believe it! The Teacher is coming down the path near me. Do I dare cry out for mercy? He has not healed anyone today, why would he want to heal me?

He could do it, couldn't he? He's from God, and God can do anything he wants to do. He could even heal my rotten heart if he wanted to do it. But, would he do that for me? I do not deserve anything. I came here thinking I had a right to be healed, but now, after looking at my sinful heart, I do not deserve anything. But he could...I know he could.

"Lord, if you are willing, you can make me clean." Oh, no! I said it. I was not going to say it. Do not look at me; I mean,

please look at me. He is reaching out; will he push me out of his way? He is touching me! He is touching *me*. Doesn't he know I have leprosy? Now he will be *unclean*. How can he stand to touch me? I am so disgusting. If he only knew the grossness of my heart, he would surely not want to be near me. But, his eyes. I see something in his eyes. It is as if he knows the grossness in me but he's not afraid. I have never before looked into the eyes of love.

"*I am willing,*" he said. "*Be clean.*"

Like the man with leprosy, we too can be made clean. Jesus is willing. He has proven that by touching our sin-filled lives and becoming unclean for our souls' sake (2 Corinthians 5:21). Whether or not our physical bodies will ever be cured in this life, the hope that we can have in Christ is that our spiritual bodies can be made clean through his sacrifice on the cross if we will believe and obey him.

He is willing...are you?

Part 3

THE LAZARUS
CLUB

Introduction

Jesus, once more deeply moved, came to the tomb. It was a cave with a stone laid across the entrance. "Take away the stone," he said.

"But Lord," said Martha, the sister of the dead man, "by this time there is a bad odor, for he has been there four days."

Then Jesus said, "Did I not tell you that if you believed, you would see the glory of God?" When he had said this, Jesus called in a loud voice, "Lazarus, come out!"

John 11:38-40, 43

Is your life and faith raising a stink? Martha was afraid that if the stone were moved, her brother's body would raise a big stink. When the stone *was* moved and when Jesus raised Lazarus from the dead, he did cause a big stink. It was not the stink of his decaying body, however. Rather, it was the stink of the faith and power of Jesus that was raised among the chief priests and Pharisees. "So from that day on they plotted to take his life" (John 11:53).

At a recent conference of church leaders from around the globe, I was reunited with some of my best friends in all the world. I was reawakened to the miracles of God and reminded of all the people that God has powerfully healed. I was reminded of all the people who were raised from near death and who, because of their faith, have become a big stink among the forces of evil.

It is becoming more obvious to me that when we become disciples, we are immediately put on Satan's hit list. When you grow as a disciple and lead large numbers of people, you become a bigger threat to Satan and to his schemes. Suddenly your picture appears on the post office walls in hell. Others move up to the "public enemy #1" slot. In God's infinite wisdom he has allowed some of his more noticeable leaders in the kingdom to get hit and hit hard. Why? Because, simple illnesses and simple cures might not show the power and love of God most powerfully or effectively. But his sovereignty is more publicized when some of his frontline warriors get hit. Remembering that God doesn't allow us to handle more than we can bear, these warriors have already been tested and proven worthy to suffer for Christ. Likewise, their progress and their cures will become more public. God turns what could be an ordinary surgical procedure into an extraordinary opportunity for a miracle. Satan would have had it end in tragedy. The exciting truth is that for a faithful disciple, even death is a victory. We can't lose.

In this portion of the book I am including true stories about some of those disciples. We have joyously named ourselves "The Lazarus Club." Most of the members have come close to death. Let me introduce them to you:

Dr. Tom Arnett of San Diego is a physician. His story is told from the unique perspective of a doctor who realizes his need for "The Great Physician."

Roxanne Armes embodies many of God's miracles. She and her husband, Eddie, serve in the church in Washington D.C. and are also directors for HOPE Youth Corps.

Erica Kim and her husband, Frank, lead the largest church of any kind in Tokyo, Japan. Erica's life has had impact on women across the world. Her battle with lupus is a powerful story of victory through the power of God.

Barry Beaty is a brother who has faced the challenge of life-threatening brain tumors. Barry and his wife, Lin, have led churches both inside and outside of the United States.

Tom Jones, the Managing Editor for Discipleship Publications International, is also an honorary member of "The Lazarus Club." Tom has multiple sclerosis, and you can read his story in his powerful book *Mind Change: The Overcomer's Handbook*, which is a valuable spiritual help for all disciples who face any life challenge.*

And the list could go on. This group is really only a small representation of the disciples who have learned the secrets of being "blessed" as Matthew 5 describes.

*Thomas A. Jones. *Mind Change: The Overcomer's Handbook* (Woburn, MA: DPI, 1995).

Critical illnesses are not a requirement for leadership, but the lessons learned show that God's leaders have been refined by fire. To Satan, the lives of these godly men and women may be raising a "big stink," but to God they are the "aroma of Christ" (2 Corinthians 2:14-16).

19

The Valley of the Shadow of Death

Thomas Arnett, M.D.

"Wait a minute...this is not what I planned for my life!" At age forty-six I had never smoked or abused drugs or alcohol. I exercised frequently, had a normal cholesterol level and a family history of longevity. Suddenly I was in the hospital with words ringing in my ears like "cardiac arrest," "life-flight jet," and "CPR." As an obstetrician/gynecologist (OB/GYN) physician, I was very familiar with medical crises, none of which involved my life or my health. I was used to saving lives and being a hero, or consoling patients and parents about disease and death, but these things were not supposed to happen to me.

On the night of October 14, 1987, I came home from a meeting at church and went to bed at about 11:30 p.m. Shortly after I fell asleep, my wife, Janet, who was just drifting off to sleep herself, heard an unusual noise from my side of the bed: I was unconsciously gasping for air before full cardiac arrest. She called my name, trying to awaken me, but I didn't answer. When she turned on the light, she thought I was having a stroke. I appeared to be unconscious. My arms and hands were drawn up across my chest, and I was breathing very erratically. Looking at me, she could see that my heart was pounding in my chest very slowly. She then began mouth-to-mouth resuscitation and screamed for Erin, our then seventeen-year-old daughter, to help. Janet then called Bill Thompson, my partner in practice, who lived down the street.

When Bill arrived he continued doing CPR and told Janet to call an ambulance and a cardiologist who was a personal friend of ours. We lived in a small town, so everyone arrived within a few minutes. After the physicians and paramedics managed to shock my heart into rhythm, start IV fluids and insert a breathing tube into my lungs, I was taken to the hospital. At some point in the emergency room, Janet was told by one of the physicians that I had possibly sustained brain damage from lack of oxygen during the arrest. (Brain damage normally occurs within a few minutes of a cardiac arrest.)

I don't remember any of the preceding events. In fact, I forgot things like my social security number for a while. The first memory I have of my hospitalization is a friend rubbing my scalp, which hadn't been washed in about a week. There was also a helium-filled balloon floating around in the room. My family says I asked about it so repeatedly they had to get rid of it. Then I remember being wheeled down the corridors of the hospital on a stretcher and into an ambulance to take me to the life-flight jet. It seemed so strange to see the solemn people in the hospital corridors who for the past fourteen years had cared for my patients and taken orders from me. Now they were looking at me—a patient!

I was flown to Vanderbilt Hospital in Nashville, and the next two weeks revealed a lot about my character and my relationship with God. I remember being introspective, quiet, noncommunicative and most of all, angry at God. I didn't want to read my Bible or pray, and I spent endless hours watching the TV screen so I wouldn't have to think. After all, I had dedicated my life to God (or so I thought). We had started a church in our home, painstakingly nurtured a congregation of about 150 people, given hundreds of thousands of dollars to God, and look what he had allowed to happen to me! It was as if I had somehow bargained with God that my "good works" would protect me from suffering and disease. Little did I then realize just how arrogant my attitude was. I was later reminded of what the Lord said to Job, "Will the one who contends with the Almighty correct him? Let him who accuses God answer him!" (Job 40:2).

I went through three or four torturous cardiac studies, which were designed to actually reproduce the arrhythmias that resulted in cardiac arrest! As I lay on a cold table, I anticipated and experienced near-death and then was shocked back to consciousness. People can even be clinically dead in these tests, which can be described in one word—terror! After these studies, the cardiologists decided that a specific drug *could* prevent future cardiac arrests, but that I would always be at risk. I also had a pacemaker implanted to regulate my heart rate. Many people have asked if I had a "near-death" or "after-death" experience, but I could not recall having had one.

I returned home to Georgia, and for the next fifteen months experienced very few problems physically. I realized later that most of my problems at that time were spiritual. Instead of talking things out and being open with God and others about my feelings and frustrations, I simply stuffed them and went on with my life.

Another Hit

About a year later, our family went on a ski trip to Big Bear Mountain in California. As I was walking back to our condo alone from the ski slope, I felt a heaviness in my legs like I had concrete in my ski boots. I also felt that I was going to pass out. At first I thought perhaps I had simply overexerted myself physically, but after resting, I realized that something serious was happening. Janet, Nathan and Erin took me to the local emergency room, where I was quickly diagnosed with "ventricular tachycardia," a dangerously rapid heart rate of 160 to 200, which many times can be a prelude to cardiac arrest—and death! I was stabilized with some intravenous medications and then sent to a hospital in nearby San Diego.

Since the availability of effective arrhythmia-controlling drugs is somewhat limited, a cardiologist at Scripps Hospital deemed me a great candidate for an Automatic Implantable Cardioverter Defibrillator (AICD). This fairly new medical device, about four by six inches in size, was placed in my abdomen with mesh; metal leads were sewn directly onto my heart. It is designed to "jolt" the heart back to a normal rhythm when the device detects an abnormality and is used along with drugs to control the abnormal heart rhythms. Janet and I stayed at the home of Ron and Linda Brumley in San Diego for a two-week recovery period, and then returned to Georgia.

Not long after my return home I started experiencing multiple discharges from my AICD—like a hard kick in the chest by a big horse. This occurred because some of the drugs used to *control* abnormal heart rhythms may also *cause* them. Two of those episodes of "shocks" culminated in two more cardiac arrests, this time in the emergency room parking lot of our local hospital. My anxious cardiologist was completely distraught as he flew with Janet and me to Vanderbilt Hospital. He was running out of ways to keep me alive, and hoped something would be available in a teaching/research hospital like Vanderbilt. I assumed that on that flight, or soon after my arrival, I would die *dead* for the last time.

For reasons I cannot fully explain, my attitude was very different this time. Perhaps God *finally* got my attention and I was humbled by all that was happening to me. It may have also been the care and concern of the couple leading the Nashville church at the time as they took us in and wrapped their arms around us.

Someone told me that churches all over the world were praying for my recovery. Instead of "Why me?" I began to think, "Why not me?" I remembered the words of Job, one of the best-known sufferers of all time "Though he slay me, yet will I hope in him" (Job 13:15). I had begun to grasp that God was really in control, and whatever his plans were for my life I must accept them as his good and perfect will, even though I couldn't understand them. I must have the attitude of Daniel's friends who said, "The God we serve is able to save us...and he will rescue us....But even if he does not...we will not serve your gods or worship the image of gold..." (Daniel 3:17-18). I decided that I would never stop trusting God, no matter what might happen.

In 1990 we moved from Nashville to San Diego to be near our children, who were students at San Diego State University. I was well enough to sign a contract with the Navy as a physician in the OB/GYN department of the largest Naval hospital in the world. This verse was truly coming to life for me: "And my God will meet all your needs according to his glorious riches in Christ Jesus" (Philippians 4:19).

The School of Suffering

I've learned a lot about myself, pain, uncertainty, trusting in God and believing he has my best interests at heart. To sum it up, I've learned the following:

1. God is in control whether I recognize it or not.

> You hem me in—behind and before;
>   you have laid your hand upon me....
> All the days ordained for me were written in your book
>   before one of them came to be.
>   *Psalm 139:5, 16*

2. I can choose my response to adversity, but I cannot choose whether I experience adversity or not.

> Without weakening in his faith, he faced the fact that his body was as good as dead....he did not waver through unbelief regarding the promise of God, but was strengthened in his faith and gave glory to God, being fully persuaded that God had power to do what he had promised.
>   *Romans 4:19-21*

3. I do not know what the future holds.

I am not afraid of death, but I must admit that I do have some "concern" about the possible pain and suffering along the way there!

> Yet I am always with you;
>   you hold me by my right hand.
> You guide me with your counsel,
>   and afterward you will take me into glory.
> Whom have I in heaven but you?
>   And earth has nothing I desire besides you.
> My flesh and my heart may fail,
>   *but God is the strength of my heart*
>   *and my portion forever.*
>   *Psalm 73:23-26, emphasis mine*

4. I have a faithful wife.

Janet has been a phenomenal support throughout the years, consoling me, challenging me, standing by me and loving me in a way that is totally incomprehensible outside the kingdom of God. I wouldn't have made it without her. The following scripture could have been written about her:

> A wife of noble character who can find?
> She is worth far more than rubies.
> Her husband has full confidence in her and lacks
>   nothing of value.
> She brings him good, not harm, all the days of her life.
>   *Proverbs 31:10-12*

God Holds the Future

In my mind I have known all along that my specific heart disease, an idiopathic cardiomyopathy (a heart muscle disease of unknown origin), would cause my heart to further deteriorate with time. After all, this was the same disease that claimed the lives of two famous basketball players, Reggie Lewis and Hank Gathers.

I had my AICD battery replaced in 1992 and this year discovered that my pacemaker battery was also getting weaker. In preparation for its replacement, I had my annual echocardiogram which showed a significant decrease in cardiac function over the past year—I had lived with about fifty percent function for seven years and now it was down to about thirty percent.

I'm fifty-four years old now and still working full-time for the Navy. In addition, my wife and I serve as a shepherding couple for our sector of the church, which also requires much time and effort.

I was recently referred to a heart failure/transplant specialist for an evaluation. After several tests, he determined that it was time for me to consider a heart transplant. Yet he admits that I am somewhat of a paradox—capable of doing all that I do with very limited heart function! I am still struggling with this decision and cannot yet say that I am resolved. What I do know is that no matter what the future holds, my faith and my trust are in God, and I will never be alone.

20

He Didn't Bring
Me This Far to Leave Me

Roxanne Armes

I have always believed that God does not give us more than we can bear (John 16:12). And I also believe that he has confidence in each of us to be victorious in every trial he allows us to go through. Two years ago, however, I felt like God must have made a mistake and that I could not possibly handle the situation in which I found myself.

I was twenty-eight years old, and I had three children, ages seven, four and eighteen months. My husband, Eddie, and I were in the full-time ministry in Philadelphia and preparing to move to Washington D.C. to be in the ministry there. One night I woke up in extreme back pain. When I urinated, I began hemorrhaging. I was rushed to the hospital and after five hours of x-rays, they finally determined that there was something wrong with my left kidney. I also found out that my blood pressure was so high that I would have had a stroke and died if they had not caught it when they did. That week while I was in the hospital, they performed all kinds of medical tests and scans (MRI, CAT scan, etc.) to figure out the exact problem with my kidney. Finally, they discovered that I had a tumor the size of a head of lettuce around my kidney and they would have to operate as soon as possible. The tumor was squeezing the very life out of my kidney and driving my blood pressure up.

I remember when I heard the news: I just could not believe my ears! Me, one of the most healthy women on the planet! The doctors explained that I would most likely lose my kidney. That worried me, and I asked all kinds of questions. The doctors assured me that they believed this was a benign tumor because of the size of it.

I had never been operated on before, and a major surgery like this scared me to death! But God showed his love for me through the support of the disciples in the Philadelphia church and many other churches. In a matter of a few hours, some disciples donated more than the several pints of blood I needed for the surgery. One of the women knew I was worried about my losing one kidney and the possibility of my other one failing. She told me that if I needed it, she would give me one of hers! Her gracious offer both moved and convicted me. She was not even a family member, but because of Christ's love for her, she loved me enough to sacrifice her own kidney to help me.

Before the surgery, we decided to get a second opinion at the University of Pennsylvania. I was able to get an appointment with the head of urology—a miracle in and of itself! He took one look at my CAT scan and said that with a tumor that large, it was probably renal cell carcinoma. He also said that I would not even be able to have surgery until I had further testing to see if it had spread to other organs or into my bones. If I was lucky, it was contained and he would schedule me for the surgery there at U-Penn. I could not even scream, cry or fall apart! I was in shock and very scared. I had gone from being afraid of having surgery to finding out that I might already be too far gone for it. I had never felt such hopelessness about my future.

During the next week, I spent every day at the hospital undergoing tests. Paul's injunction in 2 Corinthians 10:5 about taking every thought captive came alive for me as never before. It seemed like every minute of the day I was a fighting the battle to stay positive. Some days I sang to myself every minute to keep my mind on God and not to think about what was happening to me. Words of a song I had sung when I was a child came back to me:

> He didn't bring us this far to leave us!
> He didn't teach us to swim to let us drown.
> He didn't build his home in us to move away.
> He didn't lift us up to let us down.

I sang it over and over again with tears running down my face. I was so scared, but I knew that God was with me every step of the way. In my prayers I always told God that I wanted to be thankful for going through this. I wanted to learn everything he wanted me to learn and to be able to help others going through similar situations. I told him that I would never ask "Why?" only "How can I use this to glorify you?" I knew that there must be a reason why he was allowing this to happen to me.

My husband, Eddie, was such a rock through everything. Whenever I would cry in desperation, he would say, "Roxanne, God has already done so many miracles in your life. He has brought you this far, and you are too valuable to the kingdom for him to let you die now." He had enough faith for both of us.

The biggest emotional battle I had to face was looking at my children and thinking about leaving them. I knew that if God wanted to take me home, he would provide for my children, but it was the hardest thing I have ever had to face! I truly learned to put them in God's hands and to believe he would take care of them with or without me. In any case, I pleaded with God that, if it was his will, he would please allow me to live—even if it were only for five more years. It took me a while to truly emotionally surrender to God's plans for my life, but by the time they took me into the operating room the morning of surgery, I felt the peace of God that Paul talks about in Philippians 4:7.

Praise God, I made it through the surgery and the long weeks of recovery afterwards. The tumor was cancerous. I would like to tell you that I'm home-free at this point, but that is not the case. I go every six months for testing to see if any cancer has returned. Statistics say that I have a thirty percent chance of surviving five more years and a fifteen percent chance of surviving ten years more or longer. But I know that God specializes in miracles!

Through all of this, my faith has grown tremendously. It has been two years since my surgery. There are times when I get emotional, but I continue to trust that God has given me a second chance. Every day I have on earth I want to make a difference for him. I have kept my promise to him to never ask him why. Now I am so thankful that God allowed me to go through this and that he continues to give me opportunities to help others because of it! To God be the glory!

21

My Battle: God's Glory

Erica Kim

About six years ago, shortly after the birth of my second daughter, I experienced the onset of some serious health problems. As a young mother, I thought that the problem was due to having a newborn baby and a busy schedule. I felt very challenged both spiritually and physically by so much to do each day.

Finally, after a few weeks of being so sick that I could not even move, I went to the hospital for a series of tests. What I thought was a case of extreme fatigue and flu turned out to be a very serious illness affecting my immune system. I was daily besieged by headaches, blotches all over my body, hair loss, throwing up and other uncomfortable symptoms.

When I got sick, I went through various stages as I tried to understand and deal with it. At first, I denied everything. I kept thinking that I was not sick at all. In fact, people would often come over or call and ask how I was doing, and I would tell them I was feeling fine. Three months of not being able to move at all finally convinced me that I was seriously ill and that it was not going to go away with just a little rest.

Then came the ugly feelings of guilt. I kept trying to get up and do all the things I wanted to do and was supposed to be doing in the ministry. Yet, no matter how hard I tried, I could not go to church, or evangelize or help the people around me like I once did.

One day, my husband, Frank, and I sat in the bathroom together and just cried to God. I realized that I had to approach God and the Bible in a new and different way to accept the changes in my life.

One great reassurance that I received from God's word was that Jesus wanted to heal the sick. As he preached about spiritual healing, Jesus showed deep compassion to those who were suffering physically.

> When evening came, many who were demon-pos-
> sessed were brought to him, and he drove out the spirits
> with a word and healed all the sick. This was to fulfill what
> was spoken through the prophet Isaiah:
> "He took up our infirmities
>   and carried our diseases."
>
> *Matthew 8:16-17*

I knew that if Jesus wanted to heal the people of his time, he wanted to heal me as well.

As my heart began to change, God began to work in re-markable ways. After receiving great medical care, I was on the road to recovery, or so I thought. I was feeling a little bit like I used to when I was healthy. Then after a year or so, I began to feel the same old symptoms coming back. I thought I was get-ting better, but I was not. All of a sudden, reality hit me: I might never get better. There is no known cure for my illness according to traditional medical science. So, I decided that I would accept what God was allowing. I would accept the chal-lenge of being ill and become the happiest sick person in the world. I did not get there right away, but the change in my attitude has definitely helped change the course of my illness.

It has been five years since I was diagnosed with lupus. After being in remission for almost a year, I was recently pro-nounced totally cured. I am now back to doing all that I used to do. I believe that Jesus really did heal me. Most importantly, he healed my heart and my faith. And every time I feel faith-less about my health, I picture myself as the bleeding woman in Mark 5. I see Jesus standing before me. There is no crowd in the way. Then, just like the bleeding woman I think, "If I just touch his clothes, I will be healed" (Mark 5:28). I picture Jesus saying to me, "Daughter, your faith has healed you. Go in peace and be freed from your suffering" (Mark 5:34). And at that point, I do feel freed from my suffering—my spiritual suffer-ing. I stop suffering from worry, anxiety, fear and depression. I then realize that I am healed and I have been healed in a far greater way than I could ever imagine: I have the salvation of my soul.

Because of what has happened, the last few years have been a time of much growth and understanding of God's grand plan for my life. Though it has been a hard battle, I believe it has definitely brought glory to God. Though at first I did not feel so, I am grateful for what God has allowed to happen in my life. It has taken much prayer and support from so many to overcome difficult times physically and emotionally. I have also learned so much about feeling with others who are going through difficult times.

The following is an excerpt from an article on "Mercy" that I wrote in the book *First...the Kingdom:*[1]

Mercy also comes in the form of understanding and compassion. For instance,

As Jesus approached Jericho, a blind man was sitting by the roadside begging. When he heard the crowd going by, he asked what was happening. They told him, "Jesus of Nazareth is passing by."

He called out, "Jesus, Son of David, have mercy on me!" (Luke 18: 35-38).

Out of his compassion and understanding, Jesus gave him sight. He had mercy on the blind beggar.

Although I do not have the gift to heal like Jesus, God has allowed me to minister to the hearts of those struggling with illness and physical handicaps. I have lupus, an illness that limits my activity, my life-style and my schedule. Before becoming sick, I didn't think much about people with chronic illnesses or physical disabilities. I would talk to such people and even feel sorry for them, but I could never feel *for* them deeply in an empathetic way. Because of my illness the last three years, I now have in my heart a feeling of mercy and care for those whose activities are limited by physical challenges. In fact, I can understand their struggles and help heal the pain in their hearts by sharing with them what I have learned and how I have overcome feeling sorry for myself. Having this illness has helped me become more like God—to see things more through his eyes. I am glad that God allowed me to be ill. I have learned a form of mercy that I would have never understood otherwise.

Truly, the merciful are blessed (superlatively happy) because they continue to receive mercy, even as they give it—especially as they give it. The greatest joy that we can have is our salvation in Christ. It comes totally from God's mercy. "Therefore, I urge you, brothers, in view of God's mercy, to offer your bodies as living sacrifices, holy and pleasing to God--this is your spiritual act of worship" (Romans12:1). Let us worship God by showing the same mercy to others that he has shown to us.

I praise God for both teaching me and healing me.

22

What Is Happening to Me?

Barry Beaty

The ministry in New York was foremost in my mind on December 5, 1985. Lin and I had just begun leading the Franklin Lakes ministry group, which included an outreach to Farleigh Dickinson University. That evening we had our first activity for the students, and many visitors had attended. My mind was full of plans and excitement about this new challenge. In fact, we had just set up our first Bible study. That evening I went to bed with high hopes, confident dreams and much joy about this new outreach.

Then, early in the morning on December 6, I had a grand mal seizure. I never felt anything and was never conscious of what had happened. Lin somehow managed to get me to the hospital. About 4:00 a.m. I woke up in Hackensack Medical Center as a doctor was putting needles in my arm. *Where am I?* I thought. *What is going on?* It was a scary feeling to wake up in a hospital without any idea of why you are there.

Immediately my understanding of God's plans for me was clouded. My goal in life was to have a great faith in God. Yet, my faith had never been challenged to grow like this until it had to stand up under the conflicts I now faced.

The medical tests revealed that either an Arterio Venous Malformation or a tumor was the cause of the seizure. The doctors in New York believed it was an AVM. On February 4, Dr. Ransohoff performed neurosurgery at New York University Medical Center. When I woke up in the intensive care unit and heard the news from Lin that I had an astrocytoma tumor which is cancerous, I told her, "Honey, it hurts and I'm scared." Both the severe headaches and the fears that I had during my time in the intensive care unit occupied much of my thoughts. The pain drove me to cry out to God more than ever.

Our trust in God began to mature as Lin and I experienced these tough situations. Our faith developed as we dealt with the many questions that popped up with no apparent answers. Our faith was also refined as I experienced pain with no relief. Satan introduced doubts, frustrations and pains. We experienced victory, however, as our faith in God grew, as our hope developed and as we submitted to God's word.

The hospital released me ten days after the surgery. Three weeks later, I began radiation treatments at Columbia Presbyterian Hospital. The therapy lasted seven weeks. During this period, I grew increasingly weak, lost weight and began to feel more and more frustrated. I determined to maintain a positive attitude and continued to work in the ministry as much as possible to get through this difficult period. But when my hair fell out, I felt like things were completely out of my control, and I was exhausted. I knew I had to call on God for more strength.

During our ordeal, our hope increasingly grew by reading and obeying God's word. I kept thinking about Romans 5:2-5, where Paul writes,

> And we rejoice in the hope of the glory of God. Not only so, but we also rejoice in our sufferings, because we know that suffering produces perseverance; perseverance character; and character hope. And hope does not disappoint us.

Why Is This Happening?

None of us realized that my surgery would reveal a tumor, nor could we have foreseen my long period of radiation therapy. There were many tests, dozens of trips to receive treatments and a hundred times of asking *Why? Why is God allowing me to experience this? Am I doing something wrong, either physically or spiritually? Why now? How much can I endure?* As I pondered these questions, a strange thought entered my mind: *Why not me?* I began to wonder, *Do I have a strong faith in God today? Why shouldn't my faith be tested?*

As I lay in my hospital bed, I began to think of the others who were also in the hospital. A majority of them were struggling with fears and pain. Many had attitudes that were negative, sarcastic or despondent. It was obvious that their hardships were getting to them. The temptation to be controlled by suffering and fearful attitudes was a major concern I could really relate to now. I wanted to help, yet I needed help with my attitude about suffering first.

It is so easy to talk about a strong faith in God. But our strengths (and weaknesses) are not measured until they stand up against trials. These trials helped me to humbly see my weaknesses and turn to God for his strength and understanding. I thought about the passage in Psalm 46:1-3:

> God is our refuge and strength,
>   an ever-present help in trouble.
> Therefore we will not fear, though the earth give way
>   and the mountains fall into the heart of the sea,
> though its waters roar and foam
>   and the mountains quake with their surging.

Repeatedly, I struggled with the question, *What do I have faith in?* With each headache, each attack of dizziness, nausea and fatigue, I reflected over the previous months. It had been a great fall semester in the ministry in New York City. God had blessed both Lin and me with fruitful studies, strong discipling relationships and fun friendships. The lessons I had been learning were challenging and inspiring. I had a lot of faith in how God was using us. But it is easy to have "strong" faith when we are healthy, fruitful and "not in need." Studying and obeying God's commands when it hurts is the only way to develop a deep faith in him.

> During the days of Jesus' life on earth, he offered up prayers and petitions with loud cries and tears to the one who could save him from death, and he was heard because of his reverent submission. Although he was a son, he learned obedience from what he suffered and, once made perfect, he became the source of eternal salvation for all who obey him.
>
> *Hebrews 5:7-9*

Now I knew for sure that trusting in my past or present situation was not the answer to being right with God. Over the next several months I prayed many prayers involving loud cries and tears. I never imagined learning obedience by suffering physical pain. Then I learned the value of submitting to God even when it hurts physically.

In addition, I had to ask myself, *What does God want me to learn?* To begin with, I discovered one of my greatest needs was to develop a learning attitude. Learning lessons from God comes through opening our hearts to the Word and to discipling relationships. Other character changes I needed to make surfaced. Independence, pride, self-reliance, self-motivation, avoiding conflict and insensitivity were a few things that I needed to work on to be more Christlike.

Last of all, when asking the question "Why?" I had to consider the purpose of this seizure. In John 11, Jesus indicates that the purpose of Lazarus' illness was not death, but for the glory of God to be manifested. I am well aware that God can be glorified by death as well as life, but I prayed that my life and experiences would be used by God to advance the kingdom.

In my weakness immediately following my surgery, God worked mightily in the ministry group we were leading. Despite my health challenges, our group had twelve baptisms over a twelve week period, and I am confident that God made it happen. In fact, this was the most fruitful time the Franklin Lakes area had experienced. It made me think of the passage, "My grace is sufficient for you, for my power is made perfect in weakness" (2 Corinthians 12:9).

Then Lin and I moved to Manhattan. The initial reason for the move was because I could not drive for the next several years. It was frustrating being "immobile" in New Jersey because I loved the people so much and I just could not see them very often. I didn't want to move to the city. It would mean starting over again with new relationships. However, God worked powerfully in our new group in the next few months.

Making God's Priorities Our Priorities

Suffering teaches us what we are really living for today. The average day or week is filled with many responsibilities that occupy our attention, energy and time. Each week I faced the struggles of administrative obligations to the church, meeting financial responsibilities and helping people. Each of us has priorities but we need to ask ourselves if our allotment of time, thoughts, zeal and action are in all areas parallel with Jesus'.

During my first visit to Columbia Presbyterian Hospital, I met a young boy who had two tumors with one being inoperable. His parents became good friends to my wife and me and later attended several Bible study groups with us. The father shared with me one day how he had tearfully told his 8-year-old boy that he would have to "become a man" now. The son responded, "Dad, don't be afraid 'cause Jesus is hugging me real tight."

That story taught me several things. First, I need a child-like faith that is full of hope. This young child believed that God was in control of the situation. It was time for me to lay aside my doubts and to be very hopeful about God's plan for me, regardless of the outcome. Then, I need to be "tight" with God and ensure that his priorities are my priorities. Being close to God through Bible study, prayer and obedience builds the solid foundation for keeping our priorities right. I would like to share with you several of these priorities.

First, I needed to put Matthew 22:37 into practice: my love for God needed to be with all my being. It had become easy to tell God and people that I was devoted to Jesus more now than last year or any year before. But now I understood that God wanted and deserved *all I have*, not just more. I reestablished my time and convictions about Bible study, prayer and obedience.

Second, my love for people needed to be evident to all throughout this ordeal and all the tough times. I genuinely strove to care about and share with every doctor, nurse, patient or friend I met. We have a God "who comforts us in all our troubles, so that we can comfort those in any trouble with the comfort we ourselves have received from God" (2 Corinthians 1:4).

Third, Matthew 28:18-20 gives three essential commands that are linked with an inspiring promise. During the ten days I spent in the hospital following surgery, I recommitted to God my availability to make disciples, baptize and to teach them to obey everything. Honestly speaking, I came out of the hospital with more zeal than wisdom in regard to my ability, but God helped me make the adjustments. I have found that focusing on God's priorities is the key to dealing with pain, trials and loss of motivation.

Joy Is Found When We Submit to God

You may ask how joy can be experienced during these times. "My comfort in my suffering is this: Your promise preserves my life" (Psalm 119:50). When I initially read this passage, I questioned how there could be any comfort in suffering. The two thoughts just do not go together. Could there really be lasting happiness when I am hurting? I had to examine the possibilities. Initially, we must ask ourselves, *Am I dictating the conditions I want in order to be happy?* If so, there is no submission to his commands and therefore no enjoyment of his promises. The issue is: Will we let God be in control? Jesus must be the Lord of our thoughts and desires.

In discussing the characteristics of a person who is right with God, the Psalmist shares this thought, "He will have no fear of bad news...His heart is secure" (Psalm 112:7, 8). A young doctor who is one of my best friends shared this passage with me when I first learned that it is very important to be honest with my feelings, even fears, and to express them verbally to God and to my closest friends. The temptation for me and for many others who undergo suffering is to deny our feelings. We must express our feelings, but not obey them. It is easy to feel bitter, resentful, insecure, self-pitying or discouraged. Yet, we must not allow these feelings to control us. Joy is realized when we let Jesus be the Lord of our thoughts and feelings, not by allowing our fears to control us.

In addition, Jesus must be the Lord of our goals and plans. As Lin and I sat on my hospital bed the night before the surgery, we promised God and each other that regardless of the outcome, we would be faithful to God and be happy. Nothing in the whole world was more important.

> Who shall separate us from the love of Christ? Shall trouble or hardship or persecution or famine or nakedness or danger or sword?...No, in all these things we are more than conquerors through him who loved us.
>
> *Romans 8:35, 37*

Our goal was to be faithful and happy. The plan to achieve this goal was to be obedient to God, not to humanistic philosophy or the emotionally designed plans of men. "My heart is set on keeping your decrees to the very end" (Psalm 119:112). The key to dealing with suffering is obedience to God to the very end.

Joy is very possible for all who suffer if we set our hearts on obeying God daily. Think about it! We all feel happy and good when we do what is right! Let's start now.

> If your law had not been my delight,
>   I would have perished in my affliction.
> I will never forget your precepts,
>   for by them you have preserved my life.
>
> *Psalm 119:92-93*

My year of living with cancer is over. The lessons from the experience continue to provide new insight about God and my own life. God has given me much to rejoice about today. When Dr. Ransohoff examined the last tests, he found no cancer tissue or growth at all. I thank God for healing me and thank all my friends who prayed so earnestly for my recovery.

About the Authors

Roger and Marcia Lamb have led churches in Charleston, Champaign and Chicago, Illinois. They also began a successful ministry for members of the arts and entertainment community in the Boston area while Roger served as editor for *UpsideDown Magazine*. Marcia does interpreting for the deaf and has worked extensively with special-needs children through the years.

Roger currently serves as Director of Media for the International Churches of Christ, overseeing the production of news videos with Kingdom News Network (KNN) and of the publication, *L.A. Story*. Marcia serves with Roger as assistant editor of *L.A. Story* and as a writer with KNN. A talented couple who have touched the lives of many, they have three children, Christie, Michael and David.

Appendixes

In the Clay Shed

Marcia Lamb

A dramatic interpretation of a conversation between God and the guardian angel of Roger and Marcia Lamb.

WINGS: Hey God! What are you working on today?

GOD: This is that new clay jar that I told you I want you to guard.

WINGS: Nice dirt, God. What are you going to make with it?

GOD: First of all, don't be fooled by the appearance of this clay. It looks like fine clay, but there are a lot of flaws in it. My purpose for it will be revealed in the process. I plan to give it a pretty good foundation at the base, but the details will call for some intricate work. I will eventually need to rebuild the foundation but this one will do for now.

WINGS: (Reading ingredients on the clay wrapper) Oh, I see that you are using good, fertile Indiana soil as the base clay. That's good, it gives a warm homey glow to the color. Let's see...two parts Indiana clay to one part mud from the holy lands with finest sands from Egyptian wanderings sprinkled throughout. Water it down with water from the Bible Belt of America and begin kneading it.

GOD: You know, I may just make a set of these. Only the counterpart to this vessel needs to be a little tougher; so I'll start with one part German soil and one part Colorado Rockies soil as my base clay.

WINGS: Are you sure that is a good idea, sir? What if the stronger vessel falls on the weaker one, won't they both break?

GOD: Trust me, Wings! I know what I am doing.

WINGS: *(Reading directions)*
1. Work the stiffness out of the clays with relationship clashes.
2. Press down on clay with parental responsibilities.
3. Soften as needed with tender moments.
4. Pound out imperfections through son's suffering leukemia.
5. Whirl it blindly on potter's wheel till it yields to molding.
6. Shape it with answered prayer.
7. Refine the details daily.
8. Reinforce the base.
Boss, this looks like hard work.

GOD: Yes, but I love a challenge! When I finish this process, I'll let them sit and rest a bit. Then I put them in the kiln and fire them.

WINGS: Wouldn't it work to just let them sit and dry? They look done to me.

GOD: I worked with them to conform them to the shape that I wanted. They have become my true disciples. They are clean and fresh but they are not strong enough yet. When I put them through the fire, it will show us where the imperfections are and the fire will either burn out the flaws or break the jars.

WINGS: Isn't that risky? What if the jars break?

GOD: Yes, it is a risk, but love has to be willing to take risks. If I did not trust the quality of my work, I could not bear this part myself.

WINGS: *(Reading directions for firing the pottery)*
1. Apply intense heat of Marcia's cancer diagnosis.

Oh no, Master! I think she's going to blow!! I didn't realize that there were still so many imperfections in her to burn out. Look at the glowing cracks in her foundation. I hope she has the will to let go of the flaws. Master, if she blows will the other jar blow up too?

GOD: We won't know until the firing time is over. He could come out okay or damaged, it depends on his will to rid himself of his imperfections.

(Reading on)

2. Continue firing until all perfections are burned out and the jars' elements are strongly bonded. Imperfections to burn out: fear, ingratitude, faithlessness, doubts, selfishness, arrogance, pride, greed, selfish ambition.

WINGS: They made it, master! They made it! Are they finished? Her jar looks a little unbalanced, and well, frankly, Lord, his isn't exactly perfect either.

GOD: Yes, they made it. They trusted and they endured their hardships. But the process is not finished yet. There will be more fires. I have only sent one perfect vessel out of this shed. But at the end of time, when they all are returned to me, I will make them all perfect too.

WINGS: But, my Lord, they have already gone through so much. Why is more firing in the kiln needed?

GOD: Remember that I said that I wanted to make a full set. I still need to work on the jars mixed with both these clay types. While I fire and glaze the first big jars, I will be shaping the little ones too. This is a test again of how they will respond to the fire after they are glazed. They will be in the kiln glazing as the little jars go through their first firing and refining process.

WINGS: I see, so there will be more at risk if the little ones blow up. It could destroy the bigger ones or at least mar the finish on them.

GOD: Under each firing, they will get stronger and stronger. They will be able to build on the strength that I have given to them.

(Reading directions for firing the glaze)

1. Christie becomes a disciple and then becomes ill with endometriosis and Chronic Fatigue. She must learn to yield to God's will in her life.
2. Michael's chemotherapy has caused heart damage. As a disciple, he must learn to surrender his life to God all over again.
3. David surrenders and becomes a disciple of Jesus. His life dreams and talents must also be surrendered to God's will.

WINGS: They made it through another firing God! How many more will it take?

GOD: Some things are not for you to know, Wings.

WINGS: I am sorry for bugging you with all these questions, God. But can you tell me at least what you plan to do with these jars now?

GOD: I'm not sure I should reveal all of my plans right now, but I will tell you that I'm thinking that the two big ones would make nice INK WELLS.

The Moon Rain

so tell me why your tears always stain your skin
yet standing in the rain you're pale and dim
i see it in the streaks runnin' down your face
that life's become a cold and lonely place

i wonder if the stars can see your pain
i wonder if the moon controls the rain

tell me when it's time to turn back in
and we won't hide hypocrisy from sin
we'll take it to the colors in the sky
we'll take it when the sun begins to die

>   he's floating through another land
>   his compass has a golden hand
>   he's wrestling down the light. . . into your view

so tell me when his wings are in your sight
and he will come and make it all right
that battle with your bones reveals your soul
i see you through my tears and you're beautiful

ascending down among our scattered dreams
more awful than the pain inside had seemed
the fire in his hand consumes your heart
a cleansing flame of blue and white-like art

the flesh is weaker than your fighting will for life
your presence is a home-like paradise
>   you're glowing like a candle light
>   a prophet in the dying night
>   the colors of your skin are bright . . . among the rain

so tell me why your tears always stain your skin
and standing in the rain you're not so dim
i see it in the streaks runnin' down your face
your suffering has kept you in the race

the battle with your bones reveals your soul
i see you through my tears and you're beautiful

by David Lamb
a song written to encourage his sister, Christie,
and his mother, Marcia

Learning from Job's Friends

Roger Lamb

As a college student, I preached for a small, traditional country church in Possum Grape, Arkansas. I'm sure you've heard of it. The community consisted of two combination gas station/grocery stores and a church building. That meant preaching and teaching four lessons per week to people who were the salt of the earth and taught me a lot about real life. Immediately after college, I served as a youth minister in a large, wealthy church in one of Houston's most affluent suburbs—where I nearly lost my faith. You might say it was the sublime to the ridiculous. On one occasion in Houston, all of the other ministers were out of town when a member of our church died. I had to comfort the family and perform the funeral. My most distinct memory is the incredibly insensitive and nonsensical things people would say when "giving their condolences" to the family—ranging from the inane, "O my God, I don't know how in the world you can stand it," to the arrogant, "Well, I knew she was sick," to the perennially absurd, "My, doesn't she look natural." These are the descendants of Job's friends.

I always struggled with understanding Job. I couldn't comprehend why his friends were always being "dissed." It seemed as though Job was complaining a lot, and he did need to account for his sin. True friends should tell you the truth. When all these "bad things" started happening to our family, I took a journey back to Job's house and sat with him for quite a while trying to get a handle on all this. The first thing that became clear to me was that I wasn't Job. In the intensity of our suffering, nothing compared to the incredible turn of events in his life: losing seven sons, three daughters, all of his servants, his livestock and his wealth in one day, only later to lose his health. It's a scary thing to think of the little things that cause us to say, "O, I'm just like Job."

The second thing that struck me about Job was how he refused to curse God. No matter what happened, even when he complained or slipped into self-pity, he never spoke or thought ill of God. How many people can say that? Incredibly we have hurt God far more than we have been hurt, but we would be appalled if we thought God had an attitude toward us.

Then I listened with new ears to Job's friends as they came by with their "wisdom." When they were finally finished "comforting" Job, God said to Eliphaz, "I am angry with you and your two friends, because you have not spoken of me what is right, as my servant Job has" (Job 42:7). He then told them to go sacrifice for their sins and to ask Job to pray for them. Look a little deeper for how you respond to people in pain and see if you need to go sacrifice and pray.

Eliphaz: Missed the Point

True, Job had just spent an entire chapter lamenting the day of his birth. He had just lost his children, his livelihood, his place in the world and his health. Job's friends were so shocked by the very sight of him that "they could hardly recognize him; they began to weep aloud, and they tore their robes and sprinkled dust on their heads. Then they sat on the ground with him for seven days and seven nights. No one said a word to him, because they saw how great his suffering was" (Job 2:12,13).

When Eliphaz did speak it was to "preach" at Job. No understanding, no compassion, no questions. Just preaching. "As I have observed...." Eliphaz had no idea what Job was going through, but could certainly pontificate. Then he betrayed his own foolishness: "Blessed is the man whom God corrects; so do not despise the discipline of the Almighty" (Job 5:17). Eliphaz missed the point. Here was his good friend Job under attack by Satan, and he's telling Job that God is disciplining him. Great insight. It was Satan's idea to tempt Job—not God's. God's honor was on the line in front of the angels when Satan proposed that Job was faithful only because God had put a hedge around him and made life easy for him (Job 1:9-10). In fact, Satan taunted God, "But stretch out your hand and strike everything he has, and he will surely curse you to your face"

(v. 11). God did not accept the challenge to hurt his own loyal servant. He did allow Satan to strike Job, knowing that Job would remain faithful. "The Lord said to Satan, 'Very well, then, everything he has is in your hands.'" Satan took everything except his wife and even she said, "Are you still holding on to your integrity? Curse God and die!" (2:9). "In all this, Job did not sin in what he said" (2:10b).

Most often we suffer because of our own sin. There is a discipline from God well described in Hebrews 12. But there are also messengers of Satan described here and in 2 Corinthians 12:7 and Ephesians 6. Only spiritual wisdom can tell the difference. Before you comfort your friends, pray for wisdom to discern between sin, discipline and attack.

Bildad: Accused Job's Children

After Eliphaz's empty words, Job lamented again, "I will speak out in the anguish of my spirit.... If I have sinned, what have I done to you, O watcher of men? Why have you made me your target? Have I become a burden to you?" (7:11, 20). Often when we are in anguish we say things we would never say otherwise. Sometimes these are deep things of the heart that the mouth is speaking. Sometimes they are just cries for reassurance. What did Job need here? He needed reassurance that God loved him and that everything was going to work out. What did friend Bildad have to say? "Does God pervert justice? Does the Almighty pervert what is right? When your children sinned against him, he gave them over to the penalty of their sin" (8:3-4). He laid a guilt trip on Job while he was mourning his children's death! "Such is the destiny of all who forget God" (8:13). Job was still around trying to understand God. With friends like these—who needs friends?

Zophar: Defended His Pride

After a couple of rounds with Job, Zophar says, "My troubled thoughts prompt me to answer because I am greatly disturbed. I hear a rebuke that dishonors me, and my understanding inspires me to reply" (Job 20:2-3). His good friend was sitting there in the dust, scraping his skin with pottery, ruined, with a wife telling him to curse God, and Zophar gets his feelings hurt. No wonder he wasn't able to pull Job out of his funk. He was too busy being funky.

It is amazing how people attempt to comfort you when you are deeply involved in grief. At different times after being "comforted" by even some of my closest friends, I left totally frustrated, yet not knowing why. Then it clicked. Job's friends. Getting preached at. Being told God was disciplining me, Marcia, Michael, Christie, etc. Having it suggested or implied that some gross sin was inflicting this ugly pain on my innocent child. Comforters being defensive, getting their feelings hurt and needing help rather than giving it.

I was starting to feel pretty good about myself until I realized how I had done exactly the same things to other people when I didn't really know the answers but spoke anyway. I started to feel pretty good about being Job instead of his three buddies, until I remembered Job's discipling time with God. "Brace yourself like a man; I will question you, and you shall answer me. Where were you when I laid the earth's foundation? Tell me, if you understand" (38:3-4). My, how much more there is to learn. I will get wisdom if I pray for it and if I will stay close to God and his word. There I will learn how to be a true friend.

QUESTIONS:

1. What is your first thought when you hear that someone is seriously ill?

2. Do you know how to listen first, speak later?

3. Do you understand where Job's three friends went wrong?

Notes

CHAPTER 5 Out of the Mire

1. To further understand God's love see the following:

Marcia Lamb, "The Blood of Christ Keeps On Cleansing," *Thirty Days at the Foot of the Cross,* New Edition, eds. Thomas and Sheila Jones (Woburn, MA: DPI, 1993) 20-22.

Marcia Lamb, "Jezebel: A Haughty Spirit Before a Fall," *She Shall Be Called Woman, Volume 1, Old Testament Women,* eds. Sheila Jones and Linda Brumley (Woburn, MA: DPI, 1994) 119-124.

Josh McDowell. *His Image, My Image.* (Nashville: Thomas Nelson Publishers, 1984).

2. See appendix for "In the Clay Shed", a dramatic interpretation of a conversation between God, the potter, and the guardian angel of Roger and Marcia Lamb.

3. I am extremely grateful that God put people in my life like Gordon and Theresa Ferguson, Al and Gloria Baird, Tom and Sheila Jones, Dr. Hardy Tillman, Bob and Pat Gempel, Wyndham and Jeanie Shaw, and Stan and Betty Morehead to strengthen me and give me support and guidance through these darkest of times.

CHAPTER 6 In Due Time

1. *Fibromyalgia:* The best way I can describe this condition is a deep chronic pain and fatigue of the muscles. To reach a diagnosis, doctors administer pressure to the typical trigger spots. These trigger spots help the doctor to know that they are dealing with more than just sore muscles. It is not known what causes fibromyalgia. It is often seen with cases of Chronic Fatigue Immune Dysfunction Syndrome, but not always.

My personal doctor believes one of the causes of fibromyalgia to be the lack of adequate rest and rebuilding of muscle tissue. This occurs normally in the deepest levels of sleep. Reaching deep REM sleep has improved my own pain. Analgesics and ibuprofen offer a little relief. Severe cases of fibromyalgia make even human touch a painful experience.

2. Endometriosis: This is a frustrating and puzzling disease to doctors. It is an extremely painful condition that comes during the days prior to a woman's menstrual flow and even during the time of the flow. As the condition gets progressively worse, other parts of the body become affected and painful too. This is the way that Christie's doctor explained it to us: The problem is caused when some of the menstrual fluid goes into the abdominal cavity of the body, rather than being expelled from the body. This occurs when fluid escapes from the uterus through the fallopian tubes. When this fluid leaks into the abdominal cavity, the pain occurs. The body's defenses attack the "foreign" matter, thereby causing pain much like the pain experienced at an injury site when antibodies and white blood cells accumulate. The fluid then becomes sticky and glue-like, causing organs and tissues to become sticky and even adhere to one another.

Since this condition corresponds with the affected woman's natural menstrual cycle, the most popular treatment is to halt or control her cycles with hormone therapy. This is one of the reasons people say that the best "cure" is pregnancy, although that is not foolproof. Surgical removal of the endometriosis is considered when the condition worsens or to establish a clean area for the hormone therapy to begin in.

Each woman's case is very specific and very individual. Therefore, a professional's guidance and supervision is imperative.

CHAPTER 7 Hoop Dreams: Time Out

1. Thomas and Sheila Jones, eds. *Let It Shine* (Woburn, MA: DPI, 1995).

CHAPTER 9 You Are Blessed

1. Matthew 5:3, Eugene H. Peterson, *The Message* (Colorado Springs: NavPress, 1995).

CHAPTER 11 Grief That Really Is Good

1. For a more extensive understanding of the need to mourn our sins and find God's comfort see the following: "A Bright New Mourning," *First...the Kingdom*, eds. Thomas and Sheila Jones (Woburn, MA: DPI, 1994) 15-17.

CHAPTER 12 Humble and Happy

1. Gordon Ferguson. *The Victory of Surrender* (Woburn, MA: DPI, 1995).

2. See appendix for *In the Clay Shed*, a dramatic interpretation of a conversation between God, the potter, and the guardian angel of Roger and Marcia Lamb.

3. For an insightful and powerful discussion of the way Satan works and especially how he uses fear, see Mike Taliaferro's book *The Lion Never Sleeps* (Woburn, MA: DPI, 1996).

CHAPTER 13 Real Satisfaction

1. Fred Faller, "Religious or Righteous," *Discipleship Magazine* (Woburn, MA: Fall, 1991) 11-12.

CHAPTER 17 Remember the Reward

1. See appendix for further treatment of the responses of Job's friends.

CHAPTER 21 My Battle: God's Glory

1. Erica Kim, *First...the Kingdom*, eds. Thomas and Sheila Jones (Woburn, MA: DPI, 1994) 24-26.

The Lion Never Sleeps
by Mike Taliaferro

Life to the Full
A study of the writings of James, Peter, John and Jude
by Douglas Jacoby

Raising Awesome Kids in Troubled Times
by Sam and Geri Laing

Let It Shine: A Devotional Book for Teens
edited by Thomas and Sheila Jones

She Shall Be Called Woman
Volume I: Old Testament Women
edited by Sheila Jones and Linda Brumley

She Shall Be Called Woman
Volume II: New Testament Women
edited by Sheila Jones and Linda Brumley

The Disciple's Wedding
by Nancy Orr with Kay McKean

For information about ordering these
and many other resources from DPI, call
1-800-727-8273
or from outside the U.S.
617-938-7396
or write to
DPI, One Merrill Street, Woburn, MA 01801-4629